DEEP OVERSTOCK

#10: Origin of Life

October 2020

"Consider your origins: you were not made to live as brutes, but to follow virtue and knowledge."

Dante Alighieri

BIO - ORIGIN OF LIFE

Editorial

Editors-In-Chief: Mickey Collins & Robert Eversmann

Managing Editors: Ariel Kusby, Michael Santiago & Z.B. Wagman

Poetry: Jihye Shin

Prose: Michael Santiago & Z.B. Wagman

Translation: Sue Su

Additional Copyediting: Azalea Micketti

Cover: Roger Camp

Contact: editors@deepoverstock.com
deepoverstock.com

On the Shelves

Letter from the Editors

Dearest Readers,

The origin of life for *Deep Overstock* began with three booksellers meeting in a bookstore cafe with a simple idea: we had friends who wrote and did art, and we wanted them to have a place where they could publish their work. *DO* has almost taken on a life of its own now as it has grown beyond just publishing our friends' and friends of friends' work into receiving submissions from booksellers and book lovers from all around the world. But that just goes to show that the goal of Deep Overstock is a legitimate one and one that we are proud to have.

In our tenth issue of *Deep Overstock* our contributors have written for you stories about fathers, the creation of people, babies, viruses, nature, technology, and much more.

We hope that you enjoy.

Submissions are currently open for our eleventh issue: Animals, until November 30th.

Yours,

Deep Overstock Editors

The Explorer

by Ben Crowley

The Earth

The explorer climbs a dune. And at the bottom sees a hole.

The hole calls up to the dune, *Hello?*

The explorer shifts his feet. Sand seeps from under his feet and chokes the hole.

Eyeless, tongueless, *I want you to kill me*, says the hole.

The sun is very hot. There is no shade. There are only the shadows of buzzards.

I am the earth, says the hole. *It is not my nature to be full of sand.*

If the explorer lifts a foot, the hole will choke.

Please, says the hole. *Every day sand runs into my throat. It has been this way a million years.*

If I kill you, everyone on the earth will die, he says.

Yes, it says.

The Ocean

The explorer travels many nights and many miles.

He meets a captain and climbs onto his boat.

It is fascinating being soaked in rain while riding on top of the ocean.

One cloud appears above the boat. It is at first exceptionally small and bright.

I am full of regret, the cloud says.

It begins to swell very dark and very large.

I have irreparably changed people, the cloud says.

Will you rain? says the explorer.

Yes, the cloud says. *And I will break your boat.*

The Tree

The explorer washes up on an island.

The explorer sees a very high tree above a very high hill.

The explorer follows the light of the sun up the hill.

The tree is obviously the biggest tree. Its trunk is twenty times the width of other trees.

I am the tallest tree in the world! it says.

The explorer sees the hideous face of the tree. It is peeking out from under an ugly branch.

Do not touch that axe! it says. *I am the tallest tree there ever was!*

Leaves fall on the explorer's feet. He picks up the axe and loops it into his belt.

He begins the climb up the tree.

I'm warning you, says the tree. *I'll grow all the way to the moon.*

The explorer rests on the branch. He can already see the whole island, even other islands far away in the ocean. Still, the tree goes infinitely up. There is no sign of its end.

See that branch up there? says the tree. A dry leaf pops off from the branch under its breath. The explorer climbs higher and finds cuts from an axe.

Is the axe so heavy? says the tree.

The explorer un-loops the axe from his belt. He holds it in his two hands. The chunks already cut from the tree look like many smiles of much lighter wood.

Swing batter, batter, batter! says the tree.

Dark shadows settle over all the trees. The sun is setting. The ocean touches the beach and folds away from the sand. Little birds swell fat in small holes in branches.

I need to get a better angle, says the explorer.

The explorer begins to climb down. He stops. *Cover your eyes*, he says.

The tree covers its eyes. *Do you think I will make a terrible crash? Do you think I will destroy much of the forest? Any houses? You're not abandoning me are you?*

The explorer climbs down to the leaves on the ground. He steadies his feet and holds the axe against the bark. *On the count of three*, he says.

The tree and the explorer count:

One.

Two...

The tree uncovers its eyes.

The axe is there on the ground.

Nothing left to wield the axe, the tree grows endlessly toward the moon.

A Rock

The explorer wanders through many towns and many islands. He finally comes to a rock.

Tap on me, says the rock.

The explorer taps on the rock and a golden ring appears.

Go on, says the rock.

The explorer holds the ring in the sun.

But the sun is already setting.

The corner of a red blanket appears in the rock.

Go ahead.

The explorer pulls on the red blanket. And the red blanket comes out of the rock.

The explorer wraps himself in the warm red blanket and lies on the body of the rock.

I am not a rock, not really, says the rock. *One day I will be a man.*

I will too one day be a man, says the explorer.

But I will be a much better man than you, says the rock.

Internal Mycology

by Adam Stewart

"Fungi are interface organisms between life and death"
~ Paul Stamets, an American mycologist

Cryptococcus neoformans
a heavily protected yeast
that looks like kiwi surrounded
by a white halo on an Indian ink stain.

Gay men
heavily protected
with a subculture that wards off
bigotry. I am under the
microscope of religious ideology.

I breathe the air.
The ordinary microaggressions and
pigeon
droppings lead to a hematogenous
dissemination of toxins destroying my
brain
from within.

Soap bubble lesions
and cryptococcal encephalitis.
My brain burns.
I close my eyes
until the zaps
go away.
Please increase my medication
by another 100mg
until my meninges
fuse together
and I am
"sane".

I dream of escaping

to the lunar water
India discovered.
Escaping from the
religious cryptozoologists
that declare being “gay” is
a trick of the Beast.

Holy doctors treat me with amphotericin B,
fluconazole and some
reparative therapy.

Aspergillus fumigatus.
A fungal infection with
fruiting bodies: septate hyphae
and acute branches.

I was called a fruity body once.
The angles cut me sharp and deep.
I almost suffocated.

Individual humans cells
are facultative anaerobes.
They can survive without oxygen
but all together, a person (I)
can not survive.
I am slowly dying.

I breathe the air.
The oxygen is toxic.
Do I want hepatocellular
carcinoma?

Yes.

It is better than the aspergillomata.
Instead of asymptomatically suffering
people can see the horrible mess I am in.

Treat me with amphotericin B,
voriconazole and some
Holy scriptures written
on index cards.

Sporothrix schenckii

(Rose Handler's Disease)

I remember planting roses
with my grandmother.

One day my grandmother
took both of my hands
and smudged them in the
tilled soil.

I screamed and ran inside
to wash my hands.
I did not want to be dirty.
My thoughts were dirty. I
was dirty.

I soon grew out of my
Pilate hand-washing
But it was too late.
The yeast continued to
grow inside of me.

I internalized the pain.
My lymph nodes became
enlarged with shame.
I tried to pull the thorn from
my side.

Each time I pulled the thorn
the spores disseminated more and more
throughout my body till
ulcers of self-hate colonized me.

Treat me with itraconzaole,
potassium iodine and
some "healthy straight male bonding."

Blastomycosis
a fungal infection
that disseminates to my
skin and bones.

Shame is in my bones
and fire is shut-up
in my skin.

The fire melts my skin
from the inside
like a candle flame
burning wax out of existence.

Granulomatous nodules
form on my skin.
I am a social leper.
I show myself to
the priest to get
my prognosis.

He tells me
eternal damnation
or sudden death.

If the fungal infection
progresses to a point
sudden death from a heart attack
is my best option.
My soul can be saved from amputation.
The Flesh is meaningless.

I get an inflammatory lung disease
from thinking about my options.

女娲造人 Nǚ Wa Makes People

by Sue Su

在天地开辟的最开始，天上有了太阳、月亮和星星，地上有了山川草木，也有了鱼虫鸟兽，可是却并没有人类。

女娲是一个女神，她有很厉害的魔法。有一天，女娲走在路上，看到周围的景象很美，但是觉得非常孤单。她觉得在这天地之间，应该添一点什么东西进去，让它生气蓬勃起来。可是添一点什么东西进去呢？

走啊走啊，她走得有些疲倦了，就在一个池子旁边蹲下来。澄澈的池水照见了她的面容和身影；她笑，池水里的影子也向着她笑；她假装生气，池水里的影子也向着她生气。她忽然灵机一动："为什么不创造一种像自己一样的生物加入到世间呢？"

想着，她就顺手从池边掘起一团黄泥，掺和了水，在手里揉团着，揉团着，揉团成了第一个娃娃模样的小东西。她把这个小东西放到地面上。说也奇怪，这个泥捏的小家伙，刚一接触地面，就活了起来，并且开口就喊："妈妈！"接着一阵兴高采烈的跳跃和欢呼，表示他获得生命的欢乐。

女娲看着她亲手创造的这个聪明美丽的生物，又听见"妈妈"的喊声，不由得满心欢喜。她给她心爱的孩子取了一个名字，叫做"人"。人的身体虽然小，但因为是女神创造的，相貌和举动也有些像神，所以和其他的动物都不同。

女娲对于她的作品感到很满意。于是，她又继续动手做她的工作，她用黄泥做了许多能说会走的可爱的小人儿。这些小人儿在她的周围跳跃欢呼，使她非常高兴和安慰。从此，她再也不感到孤独、寂寞了。

她一心要让这些小生物布满大地。但是，大地毕竟太大了，她工作了许久，还没有达到她的意愿，而她本人已经累极了。最后，她想出了一个绝妙的创造人类的方法。她拉下一条枯藤，伸入一个泥潭里，搅成了浑黄的泥浆，向地面这么一挥洒，泥点溅落的地方，就出现了许多小小的叫着跳着的人儿，和先前用黄泥捏成的小人儿，几乎一模一样。每个小人儿都在喊着"妈妈""妈妈"。

大地上虽然有了人类，女娲的工作却并没有终止。她又考虑着：人是要死亡的，死亡了一批再创造一批吗？这未免太麻烦了。怎样才能使他们继续生存下去呢？这可是一个难题。

后来她终于想出了一个办法，就是把那些小人儿分为男女，让男人和女人配合起来，叫他们自己去创造后代。这样，人类就可以世世代代绵延下去。

At the very beginning of the world, there was the sun, the moon and stars in the sky; there were mountains, rivers, grasslands and forests with animals on the earth. However, there were no human beings.

Nǔ Wa was a goddess with magnificent magic. One day, when she walked along the road, she saw very beautiful scenery around her, but she felt so lonely. She thought something should be added into this world to make it lively. But what?

She felt tired after walking so long, so she knelt down to rest by a pond. Then through the limpid water, she saw the reflection of her face and body. When she smiled, the reflection smiled back, and when she scowled, the reflection scowled back. Enlightened by the reflections, she said to herself, *Why don't I make some living creatures like me for this world?!*

At the same time, she scooped some mud from the side of the pond, mixed it with some water, and then made it into a small sculpture. To her amazement, once the sculpture touched the ground, it became alive, and started to call Nǔ Wa "mum." Then the child danced and cheered to show happiness for its new life.

Nǔ Wa was happy when the creature she'd just created said, "Mum." She named her beloved child "People." The body of people was tiny, but as it was created by the goddess, its appearance and mannerisms resembled hers, and were very different from other animals.

As Nǔ Wa was satisfied with her creature, she continued to make more adorable small people with mud. Being surrounded by these small people singing and cheering around her, Nǔ Wa felt delighted and since then, she never felt lonely anymore.

Nǔ Wa intended to fill up the whole world with these creatures, but the planet was too huge for her to finish her mission. And she was already exhausted before she even got halfway to realising her dream. At last, she came up with an amazing idea to create people. She dragged a rusty rattan and reached it into a muddy pond, then whisked the water into the slurry before splashing it onto the ground. Once the splash touched the ground, clusters of small people appeared, and they were exactly the same as what she made by hand before. Every small creature was jumping, cheering and calling Nǔ Wa, "mum!"

Well, now, there were human beings in the world, but Nǔ Wa's work was not finished quite yet. She started to consider another situation: *What if human beings died, do I have to create other clusters of them again? Hm, that's too much work. How to ensure human beings' continual survival? It is such a tricky situation!*

After a long time thinking, she finally got an idea! She made all human beings into men and women, then matched them so they could reproduce. In that way, human beings could continue to be in the world without her intervention forever.

18 *Origin of Life 2 - Roger Camp*

Kami

by Michael Santiago

Do you remember the day you died?

I do.

It was that fateful night I stood watch atop that cliff. The cliff I had fond memories of from childhood. It overlooked the sea. The sound of waves cracked at the base as the wind howled below with the sharp scent of cherry blossoms in full bloom. The horizon spanned endlessly. This was meant to be. A portrait painted by the gods.

But behind me, my village was in flames. Our wooden houses were the perfect fuel, and the hay that laced the roof gave the fire life. Echoes of agony pierced the night. Kasuya would be no more. Our home was now in ashes.

Blood trickled down my brow. An arrow protruded out of my left shoulder and another out of my thigh. My body was broken, mangled, but my soul endured. It had to.

In front of me, my wife and child. Their lifeless bodies were strewn across a patch of blood stained grass. Slain by the invading horde, I could not save them. I could not save my people. Death was imminent. And so, I knelt and prayed to the gods as the embers of my home dissipated.

"Stand, Takeda," spoken in a soft, shallow tone.

"Tsu…Lord Tsukuyomi?" I hesitantly replied.

"Yes. Husband of Amaterasu and emissary of the moon. You, Takeda, will not be defeated just yet. You still have some fight in you. Now, pick up your sword. Go back to the village and bring me their heads. For this. I will make you a kami," Tsukuyomi persuaded.

"Kami? But I am just a mortal. What of my wife and

child?" I muttered with a confused look.

"Yes. A kami. I have been watching you for a long time. Of all the warriors in this land, you, Takeda, stand with honor, and vengeance sparks your soul. Your family will become kami, but not the same as you. For you, are bound to become one of vengeance. A life born anew. If you act out as I have instructed. Though I warn you, the path will be muddled, and an unlikely foe will present itself," Tsukuyomi proclaimed.

As I began to stand, I gripped my sword firmly and nodded in agreement. "Ok, I will act out and slay those savages as you have instructed," I said. Tucking my blood stained sword under my armpit, I pulled it out gently to cleanse it of savage blood.

"Yomi. Maki. I will be back. You will not wait long for me," I said to my family as I mounted my horse.

My steed galloped as hard and as fast as her worn body could allow. She, too, was littered with arrows, but she was always trusting. Her breathing was faint and I knew this would be our last ride together. Her tattered limbs would make it as far as the village. This was certain.

"Ha. Another to throw onto the pyre. Let them burn. They did not understand Mongol might, for this was their greatest mistake. The Kahn will be pleased to hear Kasuya and these animals are burning. He warned they would not submit. That samurai was a stubborn breed. Inu. That is what the Kahn referred to them as. Yet, they are not as smart as dogs, just loyal to a fault," a gruff Mongol spoke.

"You are wrong, Mongol. Dogs and samurai share more than you think. Fierce, devoted, and honorable. You vermin, on the other hand, are treacherous boars who see no sense in anything other than your savagery," I yelled as I dismounted.

"Look. Another wayward samurai hoping to stand against us. Why do you fight us so vehemently? Why resist? Do you see anyone around that's going to aid this fruitless plight of yours?" the Mongol responded.

Unsheathing my sword, I raised it above my head and charged forward. Slashing the throats of two and beheading a third. I pointed my blade at the Mongol that spoke with misplaced fervency. "Good enough for you, Mongol?" I spoke with a dead stare.

"No, not good enough," he spoke.

He spat on the floor and blew into the cattle horn for reinforcements.

"What is your name, samurai? I want to know so that we can share the story of the dog that bit its masters after we conquer this land," he said with a cynical grin.

"Takeda. And that name will be the last you utter," I replied.

With a swift motion forward, I severed the head of that pig who spoke so ill of our people. The Mongol collapsed and his head rolled across the ground. It tumbled along the soot from our homes like a tumbleweed.

"The samurai is over there," a Mongol shouted. My gaze shifted over to our homes that were still burning, and I could see droves of Mongols running to my position.

I whistled for my horse, but just as she began trotting to me an arrow zipped past me. She screamed and fell on her side. This arrow was lodged into her neck. There was nothing I could do to save her. I whispered, "thank you. You have been the most loyal creature. The kami will look after you as you fade into the next life."

I took out my sword once more and firmly planted it into her neck. She struggled. Kicked. But this was the best thing for her now. Her suffering and her service had come to an end.

"Samurai, on your feet," a Mongol ordered.

A few meters behind me, a dozen Mongols snarled and clasped their swords. I rose and turned around. Staring at a group of executioners ready to end my life. I was not afraid. I did not fear death. I welcomed it. With a sly grin, I ran towards them with my sword ready.

"Takeda, STOP," a voice screamed behind the men.

I came to a grinding halt and looked on. "Toyotomi?! Wha… what are you doing with these vile beasts?" I yelled back.

My brother, Toyotomi, was clad with Mongol gear as he brandished a lance he could hardly wield. He looked pleased with himself. Snickering and snarling back in my direction. He looked like an ant amid oxen. Much smaller in stature than the overgrown Mongols; he was out of place.

"There's no use for samurai in the Kahn's vision, brother. This way of life is outdated! Our country is always at war. We are always fighting for our lords who are too afraid to fend for themselves. Under Kahn, we will be unified. He has already conquered much of China and the Korean peninsula. Our island is yet a pebble in the vast sea of his dominion. This will be the new way of things for our people. If you choose to follow us," Toyotomi confidently spoke.

As a child, Toyotomi was always the runt of the litter. He never fit in. He could barely raise a sword above his head, and now he was holding a lance much bigger than himself. His brother can never be a samurai. I wondered to myself what these Mongols had offered him for this betrayal.

"There you go again, Takeda. Always in your head. Scheming. Plotting. Oh, wait… this time it was me who was smarter than you. No longer the runt. I have finally filled my boots. Never good enough to stand like a samurai, but here I am, a Mongol warrior. I led them here brother. I told them when to attack and how," he said with a smile.

"Brother, I would dissuade you from this path, but your treachery has claimed the lives of our people. My wife and daughter, your niece, was slain by these brutes," I replied.

Toyotomi began pacing back and forth in front of the

group, gripping his lance with both hands. Charging forward, he thrust his weapon towards his kin. Unable to land a blow, he got increasingly frustrated and ordered the Mongol brutes to attack. They laughed but complied.

Takeda dodged and parried attacks from all sides. He jumped back as a mace swung close to his face. Ducking, he sliced the shins of the men surrounding him. His katana moved effortlessly in his hands as he slit the throat of one foe to the next. In a flurry of swift strikes, the brutes collapsed.

"I count four. Are you going to continue to let these Mongols do the fighting for you, brother?" I stated.

As Takeda began to laugh at his younger brother, a sense of dread loomed over him. He knew that Tsukuyomi had foreshadowed this very moment. That the path he set out on was not what he would have expected.

Once more, Toyotomi, disheveled, threw his lance around aimlessly. Tired from his maniacal frenzy, he fell to his knees. The remaining Mongols looked on, baffled, and awestruck by the display. "Will you not help your brother to his feet?" Toyotomi questioned.

As Takeda made his way to his brother, he placed his sword in his sheathe and extended his hand out.

"Fool," he shouted.

A well-placed dagger lodged its way into Takeda's neck. "I should have known," I whispered.

"I'll remember this day. When Kasuya fell and the Kahn rose. When brothers fought. When I became more than what you saw," he snickered.

"Silence this dog, will you?" a Mongol said to another.

With a single swipe of a Mongol sword, Toyotomi froze as his body was split in two.

"Thank you. I had enough of his intolerable wailing. The

Kahn would never honor someone so disgraceful," Another Mongol stated.

Bleeding out. I began to tremble. Walking towards one of the Mongol horses, I placed one foot into the stirrup and rode back to that cliff as the Mongols looked on. This steed was now bathed in my blood. As it came to the foot of the cliff, I fell off. Lying next to my wife and daughter, I began to pray once more.

"Tsukuyomi, I am dying. Have I fulfilled, at least to some degree, what you asked?" I asked.

"Yes. Within reason, I will allow what transpired to make you a kami. Your life will be born anew, and you will be in servitude to me. As a spirit of vengeance. With this, your life, your new life, now starts here," Tsukuyomi professed.

"Thank you. Grant the souls of my family safe passage, please," I begged.

"Let it be so," he spoke.

As I bled out next to my family, I thought of those fond childhood memories atop the cliff. This is how it would end. This was the day I died and the day I was born again.

Bennu
by Nat PW

"From the Dao there comes one. From one there comes two. From two there comes three. From three there comes all things."
- Daodejing

He loves routines; he has many and they share a few. A favorite of hers is watching the migratory flight of crows over downtown on their shared commute home. Same time every day ("magic hour"), a reminder that the earth continued rotating as they clicked away on keyboards.

The crows fly every sunset like clockwork, bringing death, of the day, of the sun, of another minute inching by. 5pm.

Since time ticks slowly with routines, she prefers the clock hand speeding by – the faster each second, the easier to lose track.

The death of a year. A first year.

The first year together is life on fast-forward. Each kiss, each secret, flying by, losing shape, losing track.

Endings come before origins. Packing beach gear, a trip to Hawaii, she hesitates, anxious of the inevitable sadness of a flight home.

That was five years ago. Time is malleable. They moved North, got a dog, started sharing a commute in a leased Subaru – they fell into routine. From predictability sprang protracted reality, a favorite movie on repeat: understood, disengaged, but with a smile.

She became rash, searched externally for quicker pacing.

"What if we move to Berlin?" she queried. Her husband, nesting, less than stoked. Not sure what they'd do when they got there. But chaos, she says, makes time move quickly. "We're moving forward, or we're standing still."

They'd split the difference. Party in the desert. Listen to music in the grass. Up all night, then back to real life. Time flies by.

It's 5pm again. Colorfully costumed people danced and sang, unaware of slipping sunlight.

Making its rotation around the earth, the sun. The rotation of the clock, this time, two days from now: putting away the keyboards in downtown. Endings before origins.

The mind wandering to some unwritten future - work, the dog, packing, 6am alarm clock.

Free spirit, desert vibes: too beautiful to spoil with anxiety. So instead she looks up.

And she caught, in perfect coordination, a flock of crows heading west.

The birds fly every sunset like clockwork, same thing, different place, different day, all now. Content in their moment, assured of routine. Separate objects moving on their own violation, but flow in Union.

Emergent. Like an index finger touching the thumb: aware of itself. The form of the crows: originates through each other.

There are between 50 and 75 trillion cells in the body. Some only live four months. Some, four days. Like the birds, always becoming. Our cells, bringing moments into being.

All crows releasing. Childhood friends, Hawaiian vacations, dances in the desert, our selves.

This moment. This moment. This moment is the origin. The Phoenix springs into being.

She smiles, becoming.

Smiles to herself and then smiles at him.

Kisses him on the cheek.

Like light off a mirror, he smiles back.

A separate object of its own violation:

"Hey, check out those birds," he says.

Origin Story

by Desiree Ducharme

Long ago, the Universe expanded. A vast swirling chaos. The Star was pure light and heat, radiating into the nothingness around it. It gathered bits of all the elements into itself. It consumed and burned and illuminated. The light of other stars blinked at it from far away. The Star winked back and knew loneliness.

The next bit of swirling chaos was a screamer. The sphere of mostly rock startled the sun as it whizzed past. The Star made ready to consume it and return silence to the void. The sphere was too far away but close enough that the Star could hear it. It wasn't screaming, it was singing. Indeed, the Star could feel the sameness within itself and the sphere. The sphere was cold and dark. The Star flared and lit the sphere. It followed the spark of itself as it receded. The song faded but the Star tracked its own light. It could see others streaking through the void. The Star discovered the Language of the Spheres and was less lonely.

The rock-turned-comet returned. It slowed and came closer. They talked while they could. The Comet thanked the Star for the gift of light and warmth. In gratitude, it showed the Star how to call the spheres without consuming them. The Star asked it to stay but it could not. It did not have time to explain physics to the Star. It was collecting Universal Goo but would come around again soon. Then it was gone.

The Star gathered several spheres and became the Sun. Some were gas, like itself. Some were cold rock like the Comet. When the Comet returned, the Sun pulled a good sized sphere into its path. They collided. The Sun delighted in its cleverness. Now the Comet could stay and talk to the Star-turned-Sun.

The Comet lost its song and dropped a whole mess of Universal Goo. The Sphere consumed it and chaos began inside itself. The Comet tumbled around it, trying to regain its momentum but physics was also part of the Universal Goo that had been dropped. It set about trying to gather its knowledge but the Sun was too bright and it could only see shadows on the Sphere. It slowed and cooled and got a bit of a sulk on. The Sun knew regret. It felt the silence of the Moon's becoming, the pain of its growing stillness. It suffered the Moon's loss as its own. It asked the Moon for forgiveness. The Moon asked for darkness and silence so it could see the stars and hear the cosmos. The Sun could not dim. It gave the moon the Language of the Stars, its song, and grew silent. The Moon accepted the knowledge and began to glow.

Things progressed quickly on the Sphere between them. The Universal Goo was woven into the fabric of the Earth's becoming. The Language of the Stars from the Sun, the Songs of the Comets from the Moon, and all the Universal Goo fused with the very elements. It glowed red-orange and black for a time. The black cooled and faded to grey. The Sun recognized itself in the rivers of fire. The Moon recognized itself in the stone as it cooled. They saw the pieces of themselves in the planet between them. The Sun shined and the Moon cooled. The sphere-turned-Earth crackled, cavernous and crisp, it became blue-green.

For a time, the planet was chaos. The Goo was so spread out that parts of it multiplied faster than others. Some parts were lost. Some parts hid themselves away in dark places. Some parts were in the animals. Some of it became part of a new animal that created languages. One of these animals translated the Language of the Spheres, the Stars, and the Songs of the Comets into their language. They used their language to focus the Goo. It came to pass that one of these creatures entrusted the Universe with her own creation.

She spoke the Language of the Spheres, she knew the Songs of the Comets. The Mother was fluent in the Language of the Shadows and often walked the realm in-between. She wanted to share the potential of creation but she was alone. She created the Sisters to share it. She put all of herself into the process. Knowing that she would not survive to meet her children, she called on the Stars, the Spheres, and the Goo. She presented the babes to the Universe and asked that they protect them. The Sun promised to warm them, help them grow. The Moon promised to develop their minds to help them become. The Earth promised to be their home, show them how to care for themselves and others. The Goo would fill them to make them whole. The mother created three, so they could always have a sister, a friend, and an arbitrator.

She bonded her creation to that which came before. Hope spoken in all the Languages. She added the first word to the Universal Lexicon and cast the first spell. Her last breath became their first. She had only this one breath to give them her entire history, why she made this choice, the reason for their existence. She knew that in the noise of the moment of their beginning, they would most likely only hear the last word or two. She chose her words carefully. She translated them into the new Universal Lexicon. One breath, one spell, one answer, all her knowledge of existence in a single exhale. "I Hope You Love." She ceased to be and the sisters began. They were filled with her light. All of them, the Earth, the Star, the Moon, the Sisters, and the Goo. At this moment, the Goo knew Love.

Universal Lexicon

Hope

Love

Death

Life

The Sisters grew with the world but were not of it. The Sun kept them laughing in the day, the Moon taught them secrets in the night. They spoke with the voices of the animals. They sang the songs of the sea. They read the stars and listened to the trees. Together, they held the secrets of the Universe. Apart from the world, they were becoming one. In their oneness, the Sisters were growing apart. One sister ran ahead of the others.

She touched the sea first, rolled faster, drank deeper. She woke first, jumping up at the first rays of dawn. She was the first to sleep having spent herself in the day. Her eyes grew dark, warm, insatiable. One sister fell behind the others. She struggled to keep pace with the first. She was slow to start, the last to wake, she was the last to stop. She told jokes she learned from the Moon. She walked in the Shadows. Her eyes grew bright, pale, painful in the day. One stayed between them. She soothed her quick sister's sores, sometimes carrying her through the Shadows when she tired. She discovered the secrets hidden by the Moon. She conversed with the roots beneath her. She listened to the waters. She walked in the Shadows with her slow sister, binding her eyes against the light. One eye dark and warm, one pale and cool.

There came a time when the Moon followed them into the day. They showed it all the wonder and weird and wild that noisily scurried and hurried. That night, the Moon was missing. The Sisters studied the Universe they could not see before. They grew cold as they studied. The water warned them to keep moving or they would freeze. It spoke of others. The Sisters grew cold. They stumbled in the dark. The Sister Between spoke the Language of the Shadows. She called them to her. She put them in her eyes and radiated light from within. Curiosity sparked. They each tried it in turn, passing the shadow cloaked eyes between them. The Sisters explored creation in the darkness.

The Sun could not find them the next day. Their laughter did not chase it through the sky. It grew worried. It remembered the first day. It remembered loneliness before the Moon. The Sun remembered Death. The Moon rose early. They talked of Death and loneliness. The Sun was worried the Sisters may leave them as the Mother had. The Sun was late in setting. In the darkness, the Moon could hear the Sisters. They were laughing deep in the ground. The Moon called to them.

The Sisters emerged Shadow-cloaked and glowing with curiosity. The Moon could see them and they were beautiful. They told the Moon of the creation under the ground, a creation that did not need the Sun or the Moon. They sang of the life they discovered in the dark. The Moon had missed the lighting of the spark and felt cheated. They were using the secrets the Moon had given them. They were learning without the Moon. They were laughing and warm without the Sun. The Moon grew distant. What would they become? It knew doubt and fear.

The Sister Between wanted to know more about the Earth. She listened to the streams and roots. She questioned the rocks. She explored a cave. Her Sisters promised to stay close to each other and wait for her. The Sun called to the Day Sister. She ran after it as always. The Night Sister ran after but fell behind and became lost. The Day Sister went to find her, was distracted by butterflies and forgot. The Sister Between emerged from the ground alone. The Sisters knew longing.

The Day Sister asked the Sun to help her. The Sun lied and kept this sister for itself. The Night Sister asked the Moon to help her. The Moon lied and kept this sister for itself. The Sister Between knew abandonment. She could see the Sun and the Moon but they did not answer her. She called to the Earth. The Earth sent her the Shadows. The Shadows told the Sister Between of the decision made by the Sun & Moon. She was of the Earth now and her Sisters were not.

She sat in the center of the valley and began to cry. The Earth knew empathy. A spring bubbled to the surface. An Orchid blossomed and spoke to her. It sang the story of the Mother. The Shadows wrapped themselves around her. She could feel her oneness, her sameness, with her Sisters and the Shadows and the Earth. The Shadows felt it too. They became part of it. Together, they knew compassion. Apart, the Sisters discovered comfort in the Shadows. The Orchid gave the Sister Between the Universal Lexicon with hope that she would add to it. Curiosity sparked and the Sister Between remembered her potential. The Sister Between knew gratitude. Being a sister, she offered to share. Orchid asked the Sister Between for creation. The Shadows agreed to be the material. The Sister Between repeated her Mother's Spell. They named it Auberon and chaos ensued.

My Fathers
by Bob Selcrosse

My Father

My father is an outsider. One day he wandered into the neighborhood.

This is hard, to a degree, because he is likable, and I am not. He goes around to everyone's house and you can always hear his name. I stay inside. My mother stays inside. My mother draws the blinds and pretends she's not home. At night, she watches the street from the bedroom upstairs.

He is so likeable because he treats every day like a birthday. And because, so they say, he is secretly a magician.

Before I was ever born, he wandered into the neighborhood for the first time, clutching his throat.

My throat! My throat! he cried, but he was so hoarse no one heard him.

He had wandered through a drought and had finally stumbled upon our neighborhood.

Blinds opened but no one came outside to help him. He was so thirsty he fell on the street and crawled on his hands and knees then collapsed and dragged himself down the street, as if every second he was losing more and more water.

Finally, a young woman ran to him with a bucket of water and a ladle. But he could not lift his head to drink. She put his head in her lap and held the ladle to his lips. He shook his head and held his throat. My throat, he said.

He put his hands inside his mouth. The girl leaned back. He pulled red and blue and green and three-hundred other colored scarves from an endless chain of scarves inside his throat.

Shortly after, they were married, I was born, and then my

mother slowly never left the house.

My Real Father

My father has tried to leave the neighborhood. He has tried it different ways.

He has hidden the sun so we couldn't wake up. He has made each member of the neighborhood walk into his vanishing cabinet. As soon as the last one was gone, they started appearing again in different houses. It was all chalked up to a dream.

I have found him digging in the trash. He stands over the trashcan and digs out banana peels, unfinished cake, and apple cores. "Are you eating that?" he has said.

I have come to him needing emotional help before. But as he listened his whole body swayed and he had to support himself holding onto the counter.

"Are you a crazy person?" he said, and he started to laugh, but there was something off about his voice. "Because if you are," he said. He swayed so much in his middle I thought he might slide apart. "It doesn't matter."

I went to him and turned him around. It was not my father, but a raccoon. A raccoon standing on the shoulders of three other raccoons, wearing my father's clothing.

"I can't tell you anything real," he said. Then he collapsed and his empty clothes lay on the floor, abandoned by a fleeing pack of raccoons.

"There's nothing real!" they said, as they ran up the couch and out the open window.

My Other Father

We all have a father who believes he is a leper and that he must dispose of himself in parts as soon and as quickly as possible.

My father caused the first snowstorm. He warned everyone that he would do it, but no one believed him. He sat outside by himself, watching for it to snow.

One morning, when I woke up chilled to the bone, I opened my drapes.

I saw my father outside. He rolled together a snowman. The neighborhood was covered, six inches of snow.

My father waved at the children from his mittens, while they watched them from behind their windows. It was never cold in our neighborhood. We did not have coats. We slipped out in bedsheets and blankets, or holding our dogs.

What have you made? we asked my father.

I have made snow.

My father waited with his arms open for all the children, but we never touched him. He was strange, my father.

At first the neighborhood fathers all had fun keeping beers cold in the snow, and the mothers stuck out their tongues as it fell. But then, when it did not melt, it became hard to get out and get food.

"I'm sorry." My father said it every morning, as soon as he woke up.

There was no fixing my father's mistakes. So we adjusted. Our neighbor's set early alarms, came out and shoveled their driveways every morning. Some even still waved at my father. And my father, no matter how bad it got, waved at anyone he saw.

One night, I stayed up late and watched him go out into

the snow. He held an old beer box under one arm and with his free hand rifled through it. The snow had already come down fresh and he was first leaving tracks in it.

He crossed the street and put his hand inside the box. From Laura's maple he hung his class ring, blue and gold.

He continued down the sidewalk and stopped at Davy's. He put his hand in the box and let an award for medical service rest in the snow on Davy's mailbox.

House by house, he emptied the box. When the sun came out on the snow, his things glittered up and down the neighborhood.

where life began - nature

by Timothy Arliss O'Brien

1.
-waters-
We swam in the river eighteen times last summer,
The waterfalls washed our exhaustion away,
And the current carried us through our griefs.

We took the bridges over the river,
Back and forth, up and across, high skyscraper, and arms length over.

We took buses and trains,
bikes and automobiles,
But every time we walked across we could hear the song of the swift slipstream,
Singing to us like the aqua in our own anatomy.

Listen, hear, and beckon,
Yourself to thank the water,
For sustaining and giving life.
Like the trees rejoice in the wind.

2.
-trees-
The trees dance for us in the moonlight,
But we still cut them down en mass.

The trees forgive us,
And still grow back knowing it may happen,
Over and over again.

Deforestation is at an all time high,
But didn't we all learn in our early education
That the woodlands are the lungs of the planet?

I could breathe easier if you would stop chasing me,
Flirting with me in the dark.

Hidden among the leaves of the evergreens
Hoping they don't clear cut our playground,
And expose us,
So they can deforest our kind too.

3.
-forests-
I'm surrounded
By broken people walking
This broken earth.

The trees have been cut down,
And I cry in my glass of fermented fruits
from the vines
As my friends sing with strings wrapped tight across that cut
down wood.

I want peace for our mental health,
And untamed allegiance for the green sprouts from the soil.

When we return to the dirt,
do our minds and spirits heal,
Sending our demons to the sea
to be cleansed by the salt?

4.
-sea-
The deep blue sea
Is deeper than your eyes.
And I could stare into both
For the rest of our minutes.

Seconds pass by
And it feels like we haven't
Taken a single breath.

The plants take our hot lung air,
And 'fix' the carbon dioxide.
The carbons break down sugars,
Sweet and syrupy,
To create energy.

While we spend our momentum cutting the grass,

And getting lost in the pools
that create our vision,

I want you to know
I will always wash over you
day in and day out
like the tides

5.
-rivers-
A river bubbles up, up, from somewhere.
To replenish and to quench our thirst.
A slow river, a languid brook.

A river flows from the mountains,
Steady, from much higher places.

A deep river,
A full river,
Rushing yet still as glass.

Shimmering shining river.
Mirror river, under sunshine.
Warm and refreshing.

A river flows through a desert dry.
Intention past each bank,
In the arid air.
A miracle.

Rivers rushing past our bodies,
Uncontainable,
Yet fragile.

Nature's provisions:
the rivers.

Alien Boy
by E.T. Starmann

In the early stages of childhood development, well-adjusted children will come to the conclusion that they come from their mother. Maladjusted children will look into the darkness of the sky. Maladjusted children, as soon as they can walk, will cover their bodies in tin foil and run through the house.

There was a boy we called Alien Boy who lived quite differently from the rest of us. He came to class in a special suit. He claimed to speak a different language, which was silence. Whenever we'd tell him to speak it he'd focus for a long time, staring at his desk. He'd go completely silent, stare at his desk, and try not to blink until he was crying, until we got bored and turned back to class. Once I was the last to turn back, I watched him until his eyes were so open his nose began to run.

When my mother and I first pulled into the driveway where Alien Boy lived, his mother was out front taping black garbage bags over the windows which looked out to the street. My mother called her over to the van. She had not yet unlocked the child lock to the back door. Alien Boy appeared in his Earthsuit wearing goggles. He put his hands on my window, as if I were in some orbiting pod.

"I see you're blacking out your windows," my mother said. "Is it because creeps run around this neighborhood?" I distinctly remember it - creeps.

"Creeps?" said his mother.

"Yeah, are people looking in your windows?"

His mother looked at the garbage bags and duct tape in her hands as if she was suddenly surprised. "Oh no," she said.

"It's because of the light. My son is light sensitive."

It was an overcast day.

"Mom," I said. "Unlock the door."

She waited. She had his mother on one side, and Alien Boy on the other.

She unlocked the door and I slipped out into the small space between their parked minivan and our idle one. Alien Boy placed my hand in his.. They were slippery.

At school, we learned something new everyday about Alien Boy. We learned that he would die if he dried out, so his mother had made him the 'Earthsuit' to keep him moist. It's because he was often caught crying speaking his language, and was eventually given green goggles that obscured his eyes. He kept 'eggs' in his desk, which he took out periodically to rub with Vaseline.

Brian, whose father was a dead airplane mechanic, took one of the eggs and pushed Alien Boy away. "Did this come out of your butt?" Brian said. He held the egg, which was not hard like a chicken egg, but malleable, like a sandwich bag full of water. It contained an ooze. Brian popped it in his hands and it exploded in class.

Then, Alien Boy spoke his secret language more clearly than ever. "I am the inevitable destruction of the cosmos," he said.

Brian's hands covered in ooze, he rubbed his hands off on Alien Boy's Earthsuit. Alien Boy, also covered in ooze, had barely touched Brian's shirt when he was pushed onto the floor. Alien Boy felt his teeth and there was blood in his mouth. He let his hand fill with blood.

When he stood up, Brian had already turned his back. He came up behind Brian and rubbed his hand full of blood around his mouth.

Brian, inconsolable, was taken home.

Alien Boy was suspended a week.

He slept with his windows completely covered over with trash bags and duct tape, because the Dark Star told Alien Boy that he was bad. It was a black circle, a star covering one of the stars in Sagittarius. It spoke to him through his windows.

You're bad, Alien Boy. You're bad. You're bad.

So his mother covered the windows up. On the inside, his windows had both blinds and drapes, and now the outside was taped.

"Ten bags each window," he said. "It's as thick as a sweater. No light can come in. Certainly not the Dark Star. Is that a relief or is that a relief?"

I remember his house was full of eggs.

They were in the closets, they were under the beds. He took me everywhere to show me where he'd hid them.

Sometimes we could reach them. He'd put them, green and slimy with Vaseline, into my hands. Sometimes they were too far back, and even with a magazine, we couldn't get them out.

"The Dark Star told me," he said. "That the eggs were going to start the invasion. That he wouldn't let me stop the invasion and that I had to keep making him eggs. But now that my windows are dark, I can't hear him. I don't have to make any more eggs."

We stared at two eggs he held in his hands. He leaned towards his hands like he was going to kiss them. He didn't kiss them. He didn't smell them. He held them in his hands, and then rolled them back under his mother's bed.

At school, the edges of cartons of strawberry milk became sticky like Alien Boy. The buttons to water fountains, the undersides of clocks, and the backs of dry-erase board erasers became sticky like him. It is impossible to say whether the things were really sticky, but this is how I experienced them. And I believe it was the same way for the others.

He told us that he would go up to meet the Dark Star. He knew that it would have to happen soon. The blacked out windows only lasted a couple of days. "I will have to go up and face the Dark Star," he said. Brian turned around and looked at Alien Boy over the back of his chair. He began to communicate with Brian silently as he turned back around and never looked at him again.

"I am not a regular form of life," he told me. He had been pulled out of the classroom to vomit into a black plastic bag, not unlike the garbage bags his mother had taped over his windows. Alien Boy took two eggs from his pocket. "I want you to have these," he said. I did not want to take them, but he put them into my hands. They were dry, almost dry. "I have to go. I have to face the Dark Star," he said. "I'm sorry."

Origin of Life 3 - Roger Camp

Start Breathing

by Nicholas Yandell

Life begins,

When one decides to live,

After stumbling around,
Day-lit paths,
As a drone,
In motion,
Speaking only survival.

That conscious choice,
To wrest control,
Of dwelling places,
Reframe the time canvas,
Start one's heart,
With a catalystic spark,
Uncapping skin vessels,
To the pouring of passions.

The emergence of a soul,
Beyond flesh and form,
Ready to spill out,
Volumes of sagas,
Exposing inner longings,
To the candlelight of tomorrows.

The open air awaits,

Those who reject the placebo,

Untether their iron lung,

And drift freely…

Tired of waiting,
At the edge of a blank page,
With miles of blue lines,
Ready to hold the weight of a story,

Only you can tell?

Then step forward,

Grab a pen,

And start breathing.

Californian

by Desiree Ducharme

Tanning season begins in late January. The first days of midterm break are dedicated to studying forecasts. Risks are analyzed. Gas money is produced. Stories are straightened. Lies are told. The locals have not yet shed their winter suits. The sand is warm at mid-day. We bury our feet and pull it into us.

Our bodies are not yet. Limbs that were have continued beyond hems. Knees peak through white cotton shutters framed by denim fringe. Middles are filled with Diet Pepsi and Snickers. Pale and soft, we expose our most vulnerable pieces to each other. Side-by-side with our eyes closed hoping, hating, accepting, being. Someone passes around chemicals for our outsides. Coconut, salt, and surf wax. Someone passes. Chemicals race through our insides.

Mama Cass and I dream little dreams. Starlight penetrates our layers. Dermis, epidermis, subcutaneous. I can feel it in my bones. You cannot hide from starlight. It remembers the pieces of us that use to be, that could be. It embraces all, new and ancient. My heartbeat slows to the rhythm of the tide. The ocean sings to me. It invites. It lures. The siren song of the Pacific striking a chord along the 115th perpendicular in the key of the 32nd parallel.

Seagulls circle the abandoned remains of dormant fire pits. The wind hums against the cliffs. Starlight wains. Salt and sand polish our skins. Shuttered lifeguard stations absolve the State of our reckless behavior. We were out of season. Out of place. Out of time. It's dangerous, this place, this state, this being. This playground for the soul with its cacophony of existence. Swim at your own risk.

At the Boundary We Are Summoned

by Amanda Depperschmidt

Under crystal neon lights, in a darkened club on the shoals of some distant world, she dances. Her hips move like the tide and her neck extends and cranes about as if she were reaching upwards to drink from some tall hanging bloom. Her feet, though delicately burdened with sandals, clap against the floors. The club's foundation sits upon the sand; her whole world is sand and sediment dumped into the ocean to make space for apartments, condos, restaurants, and of course, the dance club. Her arms shoot out in front of her, her forehead drips with sweat. Outside the sky is clouded with detritus.

"I've never seen a person dance like that," a man dancing alongside her comments nervously.

She laughs. "I'm not a person. I'm a flower." Her eyes are glazed by the disco lights.

The man cocks his head. "What's a flower?"

She laughs again. This person does not know -- cannot know -- about the beautiful dreams that overcome her, not just in sleep. She dreams of being an anemone, a mollusk, a jellyfish, undulating and beautiful, repeating the rhythms of the tide, colored by pure translucency and radial symmetry. At the bottom of the sea she eats krill and seaweed and sunlight just like she does tonight in the club where her hands are petals and the soles of her feet are roots pushing downwards.

She disappeared once from her friends and the bar regulars -- she said she does this every so often. This time it lasted five days. She could not leave. Her feet could not bear to touch the hot sand. She put herself to bed when the sun started to rise and reawakened after midday. She spent her days on the hardwood floors and in the evening looked at the bruises on her tailbone in the mirror. She could not find a reason to leave until one afternoon when she was leaning on the railing of her balcony, looking out at the town, a scorpion rattled up to her hand and tapped her twice on the finger with its claw.

"Who sent you?" she asked.

She assumed the scorpion was beckoning her to the beach, as scorpions tend to do, and so she went without thought or without changing out of her comfies. She let the ocean water run over her like bathwater and looked out over its emptiness. The sea contained nothing. The bramble and the bottomfeeders that she dreamed of had left it behind, just as she had. The sky looked down on her through the rubble. Time on the island was marked only by the monstrous heat of the sun and the notches on human vertebrae.

She moved her torso downwards, extending her spine out and across the beach. If you let it, it will stretch. She let the arms and the legs twist around her body, circular and spiraling. There was no music, there was only the moaning of the ocean crying out for the return of its monks and its mystics, the crustaceans.

And then the noise of bustling humans stirred her heart. Their souls and bodies poured out of the nightclub doors like tea from a kettle. She retracted her torso back into her hips and her face beamed with recognition. She saw the barkeep stumble out the door and suddenly the seconds slowed. Following behind him was a man holding a gun, a pistol, like grasping a black hole with everything being pulled in. The gunman fired one shot into the barkeep's shoulder and he fell face down. She let out a scream and then he turned to her, held the pistol up towards her, his cold eyes infested with fear or hate or mania. She closed her eyes to hear the shot, but when she opened them it was the gunman on the ground, a trickle of blood from his mouth.

Shaking, she fell to her knees and crawled to the body. The barkeep was sitting up and watching her, a gun of his own in his right hand, holding his wounded shoulder with his left.

"He's dead," she whispered. She held her hand over his head, allowing sand from the shore to trickle down from her sleeve and onto his forehead. The crowd returned, lifted her up, and pushed her back out into the streets alone.

In death the body supposedly relinquishes in careful order the senses as they are no longer needed. It begins with taste and smell and completes the cycle with sight. In death the eyes open wider than ever before, as if from behind a secret eyelid, ending the symphony with a burst of great light. But at what point does the body abandon the sensation of appreciation? At what point do the dew and the reflections of the natural world lose their meaning? And does the soul take the time to repent if it hasn't already in its completed lifetime? So she stood in the middle of the street, under the lanterns and neon signs, lifting one foot up and tucking it into her chest, raising her eyes to the sky, and became a flower. Not a sea flower or a mollusk or a worm, but a new thing with roots and an under layer and a feeling of sunlight beneath the firmament of skin.

I should like to think that I, like the dancing woman, might heed the call of the scorpion and know when precisely to be summoned to a place. I remember once when the whales were called to the shore and began to walk like dogs, and the dogs were called upright by the sky and by the axis of the planet and began to stand. And the humans made the desert, and they brought it out to the boiling sea.

She told me her story over a tequila sunrise. It tasted like the mainland -- the real land, like Colima under the volcano, and a life I had already lived. And she took me out to the shoals again and we waded through the waters, and she reminded me that at night people used to see a thing called stars.

"Do you think this land started as an archipelago?" she asked me, and I told her that I don't know. The dots are fading away and becoming difficult to connect. The sky is filled with debris, the fossils of the fools who thought they could escape.

The Replica

by Erin Karbuczky

She was sitting behind the receptionist desk, reading a book about a waitress in New York. The novel centered heavily on food, and she could feel every morsel of it on her tongue. Her stomach growled and she salivated. She hadn't eaten a proper meal in days. Maybe it wasn't a good idea to read this just then, but it had taken all she had to abandon it in the morning to get ready for work, so she promised herself she would sneak in some reading. Her boss wouldn't be in until twelve. She had hours, maybe she could even finish it. And by then it wouldn't matter that she was hungry because her sister was treating her to a meal at the Italian place down the street. Huge portions. Leftovers for days if she was conservative.

But then he walked in. Blue eyes. Chestnut hair. Looking like he had health insurance *and* good genes. When the bell above the door chimed, she started to give the standard spiel of a greeting. But as soon as she saw him, *really* saw him, she dropped it mid-sentence. She wished she had a mirror. Surely, her hair was a mess. Definitely, there was lipstick on her chin.

"You put your best work in the lobby?" he asked.

"Huh?" He'd pointed at her. Was he flirting?

"The painting behind you. it's gorgeous."

Oh. "No, it's not. I made that."

It was how she got the job. These days, you had to have more than credentials – experience (the right kind), education (the best kind), and the extras (internships, study abroad). She had none of those things. Technically, she wasn't even qualified to work at the art gallery. But she'd been desperate. The night before the interview, drunk and not a little high, she made the painting. Purple, orange, and gold paint splashed across a black background. It was gauche. It was garish. It was *perfect*, the director had said, and he hired her on the spot. It was terrible pay, but the work was easy and the hours were great. So, sometimes she didn't eat. She could live with that.

"How much?" the man was asking.

"Hm?" she said, sipping her Dunkin Donuts.

"The painting. Six figures?" He leaned in "*Seven* figures? I could do four million. That's the highest."

She snorted her iced coffee out through her nose.

"Sold," she said, even though the painting was now property of the gallery. "I'm Ramona."

"I'm David."

Hours later, Maggie arrived to take Ramona to lunch. She was gone, along with the painting that hung behind the desk.

The story goes that boy meets girl. They fall in love, or, he rescues her.

Marriage, babies, bed death, real death, and then some freedom before the widow(er) dies. Not so for David and Ramona. They would be each other's own personal hell. But we do not have two hour's traffic here. I've told you the beginning and I'll tell you the end. The middle is long and we'll have to take shortcuts.

See: A terrible misunderstanding, or a trio of liars.

Maggie lies for Ramona.

David lies to Ramona.

Ramona likes to say she lies for self-preservation, but really, she just lies.

It starts with a trip to Tobias, months after the tragic loss of a much-wanted child. When Ramona tells Maggie where she's going, Maggie balks.

“Like *Marionetts, Inc.*,” she said with a flat voice. “The story we read in school.”

“You don’t believe me? Come and see for yourself!”

The next day after that, Margaret was there, with Riley, her son, on her hip.

At lunch, Riley dipped his fries in ketchup and painted the paper place mat until it was soggy wisps of paper. Every coo, every cry he made went straight through Ramona like *she* was the soggy paper.

“I’m just saying, you aren’t scared? That man is the stuff of nightmares.”

“Maybe once, but now he’s the key to my dreams.”

“How will you explain it when David comes home and there’s a…”

“A baby.”

“You’ll get it in a few weeks. That’s not even enough time for you to have recovered, gotten pregnant, and given birth. Even if David goes along with your plan, you know the neighbors will question it.”

“Who are you? Mom?” Ramona hold up two fingers for two more margaritas. She would not be talked out of it now. She was in too deep.

On a nondescript Tuesday morning, the package arrived. She was startled, as if it were a surprise. How her heart quickened with the doorbell rang! Her anxiety threatened to burn a hole in her chest. “Thank you!” she shouted to the driver as he walked down the driveway back to his truck to deliver his other packages. She wondered how many other babies he had in his vehicle. He might have been a stork.

She brought the package to the coffee table and set it down. She eased the scissors through the slit lined with tape and flung aside the cardboard flaps. She started to weep when she saw it, a symphony starting up in her ribs, filling the hole of dread. Inside the package was the most realistic non-baby she'd ever seen. Swathed in a pink onesie, the overhead light trembling on its glass blue eyes. The nursery, fully outfitted cradle and all, would be unoccupied no longer. The baby was here.

Now, David would have to stop begging her to "dismantle the shrine."

Now, she was buzzing with wholeness.

"Are you sure he's here?" Maggie asked. Ramona pointed toward the flickering candle on the desk. In the illuminated room, jars of eyes, legs, arms, and torsos of every color littered the wooden shelves behind the desk, while fully put together babies stared at them from behind their glass cases. They were as terrifying as they were realistic. And then, where just a second ago there was nothing, Tobias appeared behind the till, through the purple velvet curtain which was now fluttering behind him.

She held out a hand and introduced herself. "Ramona. And this is Margaret, my sister."

"That's not one of mine, is it?" Tobias interrupted, pointing at sleeping Riley.

"Definitely not," answered Margaret, and she moved to put space between them. There was a flicker of understanding in Tobias' eyes and he turned to face only Ramona, as if I were the only person in the room.

"When did it happen? The loss."

"Very recently."

"Too recently," Margaret said under her breath.

"Excuse me," Ramona said to Tobias and turned to her. "I thought you were on my side."

"I always am," she said. "But I don't always agree with you. I'm here to support you, but..."

"Do you have photos?" Tobias inquired.

Ramona opened her purse and produced a packet of drugstore prints, "These are the only photos I have. Please return them to me when you're done."

"Six weeks," he said in return and turned once more toward the purple curtain.

"How much?" she called out, but he didn't say a word. Bill me later, *she thought. Satisfaction and curiosity tumbled like butterflies in her stomach.*

Upon its arrival the box was empty of photos, but Ramona had forgotten them. Tenderly, she slipped the baby out of the box and removed the cheesecloth that protected it from dust and damage. It looked exactly like the real Esme, dark wisps of chocolatey brown hair covering the forehead. The skin was pale, almost translucent, revealing blue veins. Quintessential pink rosebud lips. The cat came to see the baby, but recoiled when it caught sight of the thing, an uninvited alien. Ramona reached out to pet her, but she trotted away, wailing through the halls howling like a wolf until she was too far away to hear. Ramona picked up the baby and brought her to the nursery and laid her down in the crib.

David came roaring into the house. Almost delirious from today's activities, Ramona came toward him, laughing. "Do you have a fever?" he asked. David had taken to speaking in a flat, grim voice. His sadness came with anger bubbling under the surface like a snake rattling its tail.

Ramona shuddered. She hadn't prepared him for the replica, and now she wasn't sure how she would. She busied herself making dinner, while she worked through her latest painting in her head. Once she had surrendered to the probability that she would never amount to anything, creativity flowed freely through her veins. When judgment flew out the door, freedom breezed in.

"Looks good," David spoke at the meal instead of to his wife.

“I need to talk to you,” sad Ramona at the same time. Her presence annoyed him, his scared her. “At dessert.” She bought them both time. The wound of loss had not yet scabbed over. Whoever imagined as they said their vows, the territory two people could tread? “Sickness” and “health” were broad words loosely interpreted.

As dessert dwindled to an end, David looked at her. “What’s the surprise?”

“What?” She barely registered the man ahead of her, shaking in and out of focus like a hologram. There was a lump in her throat. For a moment, he loved her. He took her chin in his hand and moved her face, as if he were about to kiss her.

“I have a lot of work to do,” he said after a spell, and went to his study, where he often spent another eight hours after work, undoing and redoing the day. She took out her confusion on the dishes, and then settled in the living room with her journal, eventually falling asleep. For a few hours, there was silence. Maybe even peace.

At the witching hour, she heard the unmistakable cry of a newborn. Probably, she thought in a stupor, it belonged to one of the neighborhood girls – *women* – who were always having babies. They taunted her, pushing them in prams proudly, bearing almost no traces of exhaustion on their pristine, made-up faces, looking like French women in stylish clothes and effortlessly coiffed buns.

Just as she was about to fall asleep again, another cry rang out. This time, she knew it was coming from within her own house. She stood carefully. The floor was cold and creaky beneath her feet, and she did not want to disturb David. She crept down the hall, the cat following closely at her ankles. The closer she was to the baby’s room, the louder the cries became. Ramona darted into the nursery. Something was whimpering in the crib. The pit in her stomach expanded to her throat. Her chest was tight, her eyes welled up. Inside the crib the baby squirmed and fussed. Reaching inside, she felt a calm wash over her. She pulled the replica out of the crib and sat on the rocking chair. In a dream state, she began to sing.

Her song was interrupted by the door swinging open. "What the hell is this?" David demanded from the doorway.

"Isn't she beautiful?" is all Ramona said.

David pounded on the wall behind her with his fist, his first display of passion in months. The screams of the baby grew louder, as if through a surround sound system. And then David began to cry, his sobs extending out over the baby and his wife. She had wanted the baby so badly it almost killed her. She didn't realize he was broken, too. He had begged her to have an abortion when it became clear their baby wouldn't live. She'd refused, and gave birth anyway, the pain of which she never imagined could befall one human being. It was the pain of the whole world.

There were tears in the eyes of the baby in her arms, now. *But this baby isn't real*, she told herself. A disembodied voice only she could hear whispered back, "It's as real as you make it."

In one swift movement, David stepped towards his wife and grabbed Esme with his meaty hands. He ran to the window, flung open the screen, and held the baby above the street. Now, he was laughing.

"Catch!" he screamed to a figure below. Ramona watched in horror as Esme flew through the air, landing in the arms of a stranger on the street. She didn't care that she was in her pajamas, half naked under her thigh length robe. She flew down the hall, unlocked the door, and ran into the road.

"Give me my baby," she screamed at the unwilling participant in this war. The person held tightly to the baby as Ramona tugged. She pulled hard enough that she released the replica but overestimated her own strength. The baby flew out of the stranger's hands and into the middle of the road. A car, unknowingly driving through a crime scene, ran over the baby as it rounded the corner.

Ramona ran to grab Esme, who was now missing an eye.

David walked over from the porch and put his arm around his wife. "You're having a meltdown. I'll take care of you."

I'll take care of you, she thought, and made a plan. The next morning, she would be extra affectionate with him. Not too affectionate, as to not make him suspicious, but just enough to make him feel safe, normal again. Then, when he was fast asleep in the night …

David's eyes fluttered as he breathed deeply, sleeping hard. Ramona almost felt bad, almost stopped herself, until she remembered her baby flying into the street. Getting hit by the car. Dying. Twice ripped from her arms. She couldn't stand it. She would hurt David in the most feral way she could come up with. She gazed down at her red nails in the moonlight, talons really, stilettos. They were bright, cheerful. So was she, as she took her left hand and placed her pointer and middle fingers over David's eyelids, pressing down. In her right hand was the knife which she plunged into his heart over and over. He didn't even scream.

The shop was dark when she pounded on the door, hoping Tobias was the type to live above his storefront. He was creepy, but creepy and shady was exactly what she needed right now. BANG BANG BANG, on the door. *Please*. She couldn't afford for anyone to hear her. To question her. How did a tiny woman like you carry your dead husband down the stairs, into the garage, and sit him in the car like a crash test dummy, and drive at warp speed to Tobias' replica shop at midnight? People gain extraordinary strength in times of need, she would say. A mom holds a car in the air to rescue her child. Ramona carried her husband down the stairs to not be charged with murder. It's all the same.

David was in the car still when Tobias came to the door.

"Stop pounding," he said. "You're going to wake them!"

"Wake who?" Ramona asked. The other buildings in the

area were shops as well. The owners couldn't *all* live above their stories. But then she saw what he was referring to. Dolls stirred in the windows of his shop. Sweet, sleepy-eyed little babies.

"What is it that you need at this hour?" he prompted.

She pointed to the car with the key, hit the unlock button, and the lights flooded on. David, eyeless, stared ahead in the darkness.

"Do you make husbands too?"

Tart-but-shitty

by Desiree Ducharme

All creatures make calculations to survive. Ants calculate the amount of food that needs to be stored for the colony to survive the winter. Squirrels calculate advanced trajectory as they leap from tree to tree. They don't teach their young to make advanced calculations, they just do it. Humans need the calculations, the classes, and a way to quantify it. It could be a design flaw. It could also be the Universal Goo's way of hobbling a species so filled with the forces of destruction. Humans are a tiny, short-lived species by Universal Standards. Once they discovered this, their stardust infused egos confused "limitation" with "challenge" and they set about proving they could have just as much impact on the universe as their spherical ancestors. Since the sun provided them with a constant, they began quantifying things using the sun as their base. There is no accurate record of the first time a human quantified how productive they were during their daylight hours. It probably happened after an unsatisfying dinner of grubs and berries. One human, frustrated and hungry, does some survival math and creates the first schedule with productivity goals.

Uuk spent from star-rise to small-shadows following a hoofed creature through meadows and trees. It stopped long enough for Uuk to throw a rock at it. The rock was ineffective at making it into food for Uuk. Ukk claimed this was how you make other creatures into food. So far, Uuk had only been able to make them run. Clearly there was a design flaw in the rock. Frustrated at the loss of several meals (stupid rock), Uuk spent from small-shadows until low-light gathering and eating berries. Uuk was not the best at survival math and remembered too late that Ukk and Nuk also needed to eat.

Uuk returned to the cave and presented the handful of berries. Ukk recognized the berries as tart-but-shitty. Tart-but-shitty berries can be eaten, but only in small quantities, like a handful. Then they live up to the name. Ukk felt it was necessary to point this out to Uuk. Uuk thought this was unnecessary and overly critical of the work that Uuk put into gathering them. Uuk presented his flawed survival math (Uuk was no longer hungry since Uuk ate berries). Ukk, felt perhaps Uuk suffered from a design flaw, like Nuk.

Ukk spent the day turning over rocks and logs hunting for grubs and taking care of Nuk. Ukk did not snack while doing this. Uuk recognized the grubs as yuck-bugs. Yuck-bugs can be eaten but they taste like yuck, hence the name. Uuk felt it was necessary to point this out to Ukk. Ukk felt this was unnecessary and overly critical of the work that Ukk put into gathering them. They were pretty deep into the argument when the berries incapacitated Uuk, causing him to spill yuck-bugs into the fire. They put the argument on hold during Uuk's evacuation of the tart-but-shitty berries.

Ukk did some quick survival math. The time of cold and scarcity were almost upon them. Nuk was larval and a burden. Uuk was proving to be as well. Ukk picked now crispy yuck-bugs out of the embers and ate a few. It was crispy yuck-bug or hunger because there was no way Ukk was eating tart-but-shitty berries. Turns out, crispy yuck-bug is pretty delicious. Survival math got a bit easier as Ukk thought about the supply of yuck-bugs the area and how many each of them needed to survive. Uuk really liked this plan but continued to pick berries if they happen to be out there. Ukk tried to explain that all the berries in the area were tart-but-shitty berries which they should not eat. Uuk was not good a survival math.

Ukk was able to adjust their own productivity to account for Uuk's miscalculations. How did Ukk get here? Was this all there was? Is this success? Turns out it was because Ukk and Nuk survived that winter. Uuk was bad at survival math. He kept adding tart-but-shitty berries to his crispy yuck-bugs. Ukk was unsure if this was a design flaw or a perk.

Fever
by Dianah Hughley

The impending arrival of the baby is thrilling; it's been so long without a baby in the family. The parents, the kids, the aunties and uncles, the cousins, and the grandparents are beside themselves with anticipation. When she finally comes home, born on Thanksgiving Day, the baby feels like a gift, like a blessing.

The family chooses her name together; each voting for their favorite. The brother is 10 years old and the sister is 14 years old. They feel included; like this is their baby, too.

She's an easy baby. She eats well, she sleeps well, she loves people. She's darling. The brother and sister adore and dote on her. They play with her for hours and can always make her smile. She lies on the couch with the father every evening; seemingly content to watch the nightly news with him. The father announces that the baby's first word is "maylee' -- the name of her imaginary friend. The mother wakes up at night to nurse the baby and it feels like an island of bliss. She's exhausted, but she jealously guards these nights with just the two of them. The extended family falls in love with her; always visiting, always wanting to hold her. The grandmother holds the baby on her lap and kisses her fat little hands over and over. The grandfather flies her around like an airplane.

The baby is 9 months old when she gets sick.

June 1965

She is sick for six days. Her fever is above 104° for four days. The doctor says she has a double throat infection: both bacterial and viral. He gives her an antibiotic injection and a prescription for phenobarbital.

Then she is well, and again her normal sweet, funny self. She's talking a lot and using many more words. The family is relieved; the long stretch of fever days was worrying. The mother feels a ball of anxiety melt off and roll away. The relief is palpable. A week later, the top layer of the baby's skin on her fingers and toes bubbles up and peels off.

July 1965

Then she is sick with fever again. Baby aspirin doesn't help. The doctor tells the mother to bathe her in a cool bath. It doesn't help. The doctor says to put ice in the bath, which they do, but it doesn't help. The baby screams in the freezing water. Her face is beet red; her feet are discolored -- purple and blotchy. The brother is called to bring in more towels. He finds it too disturbing to see the baby like this; he leaves the bathroom and swallows down his roiling fears. The baby's fever spikes to 105.5°. The sister is called to bring in more ice. As she comes in, the baby's eyes roll up into their sockets -- the sister can only see the white part of the baby's eyes. The baby's limbs stiffen and she jerks rhythmically. She's having convulsions; not one, but one after another after another. The sister leaves the bathroom and leans into the wall, face first, tears streaming. She can't breathe. When the brother asks her what happened, she doesn't want to tell him. She doesn't want him to feel the way she feels. The father puts his thumb in the baby's mouth to keep her from swallowing her tongue, which is protocol in 1965. The baby bites the father's thumb with her new sharp little teeth. The father bellows. The father and mother look at each other and pull her out of the bath; dry her off and dress her quickly. The mother tamps down her rising hysteria. They get into the car and drive to the hospital. Later, when the sister sees the baby in the hospital, she is wearing only her diaper and is lying directly on ice. Her skin mottled and red; the baby screams. She has a throat infection and an ear infection. Her feet are still oddly discolored and swollen; her legs stiff. The doctor tests her blood, which is normal, and tests her urine, which is positive for protein. They send her home with a prescription of sulfa and chloromycetin A week later the baby's fingers and toes peel again.

The baby won't go to sleep without a pacifier. The family is constantly searching the house for them. They dig them out from between the couch cushions or under the bureau, covered in dog fur and dust. The brother and sister are put on pacifier duty; making sure there is a clean one available at all times. They finally attach one to a ribbon and put it around her neck. The father says it is her rosary.

September 1965

The fever comes again. Seven days of fever between 103.6° and 105°. She has a rash on her stomach. Her lips and mouth are bright red. She cries continuously. The doctor says she has an ear infection and lances her ear. He starts her on antibiotics on the second day of her fever, and by the seventh day, he is puzzled by the lack of response to treatment. He gives her an injection of terramycin. A week later the baby's toes and fingers peel.

The mother begins to keep meticulous notes about the baby's illnesses. When the baby is sick, she takes her temperature several times a day. She gives her several cool baths a day, sometimes 7 or more. The mother logs every temperature, every dose of medicine, every indication of pain, every bath, every change in disposition, every change in sleep, every change in appetite. She logs the number of days each illness lasts, and the number of days between each illness. She logs the average temperature for each illness, and the average temperature of all the illnesses combined. She begins to compile the symptoms at each stage and how they progress. The mother is adamant that everyone logs every bit of information on the chart. They do. When she shares this with the doctor, she is ignored.

October 1965

Four days of fever over 103.7°. The baby is keyed up, high strung, nervous, fretful. She can't sleep, she won't eat. When she finally takes the bottle, she vomits immediately. At night, she wakes every 10-15 minutes with violent pain. The family can do nothing but hold her. She screams if she's moved at all. The brother and sister are awakened in the

night to help with the baby. While the brother fixes the bottle, the sister holds the baby but she can't keep her eyes open and falls asleep; the brother takes the baby. In the morning, the sister remembers and feels worthless. The mother and father are both overwhelmed and they argue. The doctor gives her oxytetracycline and phenobarbital. The baby's fingers and toes peel again.

November 1965

The doctor says the baby has no infection, but her fever is steady at 103.4° to 104.2° for five days. She is hysterical. She has cold sweats; her face is chalky pale but her cheeks are bright red. The whites of her eyes are pink. Her mouth and throat are deep red. Her tongue is coated in a white substance. The doctor says it's thrush. She seems to have leg pain. She won't eat; she's very cross. The doctor prescribes nembutal and phenobarbital. A week later her finger and toes peel again.

As she grows into a toddler, she is a happy, funny thing when she's not sick; so sweet, so smart, so loving. She giggles often. She keeps her kisses in her training pants; she pulls one out of the waistband and puts it on her lips before bestowing a kiss. She keeps her hugs around her neck; pulling them around her shoulders like a scarf before embracing. There are only so many to go around, but she isn't stingy with them. She plays tough, asking "Wanna fight?" She juts out her jaw, tightening her top lip; trying to look fierce. She balls up her small fists and waves them around like a boxer; the brother and sister always say yes. She walks on her tiptoes; no one knows why. She loves her dog, Bowser. She sits over the heater vent with him and they cuddle. Bubble baths are her favorite thing -- often Bowser keeps her company in the bathroom. She loves going to her grandparents' house and they adore her. She plays with the black and white magnetic tricky dogs, and a chorus of golden angels holding tiny musical instruments.

February 1966

This fever is between 103° and 104.6° for four days. The

toddler cries uncontrollably. The mother asks her where it hurts. She points to her throat, her feet, her hand, her chest. The toddler won't take the baby aspirin, no matter how the mother disguises it. She's continuously thirsty. She wakes every half hour at night. She won't take a bottle; she only wants water. On the fourth day, her fever suddenly drops to 96°: considerably below normal. The parents wonder if their thermometer is broken. Like clockwork, her fingers and toes peel again.

She begins to talk about a quartet of imaginary friends: OrangyPinky, HonJohn, FlowerShower, and HoonkaPoonka. Somehow they live in the mother's clothes closet. The brother and sister love to talk to her about her friends, but the toddler withholds a bit. She's hesitant and protective of her friends; they are special.

March 1966

Five days of fever over 104°. The toddler's face is pale again with bright red cheeks. Her skin is cold, clammy and dotted with tiny beads of sweat. Around her red, swollen mouth, the skin is blueish. She's suddenly extremely frightened; trembling all over. She seems very insecure. She calls for each family member to hold her; one person after another. The mother gives her phenobarbital and baby aspirin. The mother takes her to the doctor, but he can't remember which patient she is. The mother reminds him of previous illnesses and the hospital stay, but he doesn't remember. He doesn't understand why the mother has brought her into the office. He asks her to come back when it's more worthwhile. On the 5th day, her fever drops to 94°, again way below normal. The peeling starts again.

The toddler and the mother lay on the mother's big bed with the window open, sharing a picture book. The day has been warm and sunny but a storm begins. Every time the wind blows, the curtains fly up and a fine mist of rainwater sprays them through the mesh screen. The toddler shrieks and giggles. The mother wants to safeguard this rainy day forever.

April 1966

The fever comes again; 103.3° to 104° for six days. She has a constellation of canker sores in her mouth and down her throat. She's very thirsty, but it's excruciating to swallow. She can't walk or stand. She explodes if anyone touches her feet. Her chest hurts, her head hurts. Her hands tremble like she's nervous. The mother gives her sulfa and phenobarbital. Her fever drops precipitously and she screams in pain if moved. When it's over, the peeling starts, of course.

May 1966

The fever comes. She vomits again and again. Her feet hurt; her chest hurts. She's wound up and extremely cross. She's very thirsty and cries when anyone takes her cup of water away to refill it. She wakes up repeatedly with nightmares. The mother gives her baby aspirin every two hours along with nembutal. The brother and sister are again awakened in the night to help with the screaming toddler. The peeling starts, as usual.

The days are warm and the house is open: all the windows and doors. The toddler dashes out the side door and something catches the edge of her sight. She turns back and looks up. There is an explosion of purple above and around her, hanging down in cones. She runs her hands through the delicate flowers, breathes in, and rubs her face in them; she grabs two handfuls of torn, bruised blossoms for her mother.

June 1966

Four days of 103.2° to 104.8° fever. Her feet are sore and swollen and the purple blotches climb halfway up her shins. She cradles her head in her hands and cries. Her eyes are pink; her mouth is red; her face is tinted blue. She won't eat, she won't nap, she lies on the couch, lethargic. The family gives her 8 baths throughout the day to try to bring down her fever. The mother gives her baby aspirin and nembutal around the clock. She's very subdued. Her fever suddenly drops to 96° and she shakes without stopping. It's no surprise when her fingers and toes peel again.

At the 4th of July picnic, she races around the grandparents' yard and pretends to climb the cherry tree. She is delighted when she spies a green snake in the flower bed. She hops on her tiptoes and chases the striped croquet balls. She wants seconds of her mother's potato salad. She's mesmerized by the red flowers in the yard, but is startled when she finds a bug in one. The grandmother makes her a summer top out of a hand-towel and a ribbon because it's too hot to wear her heavy dress; she wears the hand-towel-top with her training pants.The grandfather holds her on his lap and lets her pretend to smoke his corncob pipe in between bites of frosted ginger cookies.

The brother and sister show the toddler the raspberry bush, hanging with pink fruit. When they pop one into her mouth, the toddler's eyes open wide and she lets out a squeal. They pick every ripe berry and put them in a bowl with milk and sugar. The toddler eats every bite, then pulls on their arms, begging them to return to the now-naked bush.

September 1966

The fever comes with thrush again and stays for seven days. Her mouth is coated in white, continuing down her throat. Her legs are stiff and swollen. She's unsteady on her feet and drags her left foot as she walks. She has a rash on her stomach, groin, and underarms. She's doubled over with stomach pain. She won't allow anyone near her feet. She wakes up at 5am in pain or delirium, or both: talking to someone who isn't there. The mother gives her phenobarbital and sulfa. Her temperature plummets to 94° and her lips are blue. Her finger and toes peel again.

The medical bills accumulate into a teetering tower. The family is wrecked. The parents can barely cope. When will it stop? Will she ever be normal? Is she going to die? They are desperate for answers. The house is somber and the tension is crushing. Then she's well again, and their fears slightly recede. Then she's sick again and the weight of it is unbearable. The parents hide nothing from the kids; how can they? The brother and sister feel a creeping dread; an awareness of something beyond horrible. The claws of fear dig deeply. The doctors have no answers and the family has no relief.

October 1966

Six days of fever: 102° to 105.6° and it brings convulsions again, for which she's given ice baths. The father puts a blue toothbrush in her mouth this time instead of his thumb. Her hands and feet are covered with purple blotches, as well as her groin and underarms. Her face is white and she looks wild. She has violent chills and wants to be held. She's unsteady on her feet and falls frequently, leading to tantrums. There's a large brown patch on her tongue, and her eyes are pink. She has screaming fits that last over 5 minutes. When her fever won't come down, she's taken to the hospital, to be again laid on a bed of ice. The mother watches as the doctors carry her away, down the hallway, wondering if she'll ever see her daughter again; pain blooms in her body and she holds her breath. The doctor gives injections of terramycin, oxytetracycline and sulfa. The toddler's temperature drops to 94°. She comes home from the hospital and then the peeling starts.

The mother is devastated. The father feels helpless and is continuously exhausted; working two jobs because the mother misses so much work. They argue. The brother and sister are stunned into silence by everything they've seen; too young to know how to process their terror, their heartbreak. The grandparents hold hands and stare at each other -- just a whisper of shaking heads -- but neither one is foolish enough to speak about it out loud.

The family brings home a Christmas tree. The toddler is spellbound by the ornaments, the tinsel, the tiny houses. Bowser leaps up in excitement and the tree falls over, breaking the fragile ornaments and spilling water on the carpet. The toddler shrieks, dances away from the mess on tiptoes and dissolves into giggles. The father puts the dog outside.

The monthly sicknesses continue for years. The doctors have no idea what is wrong with her. The family always hopes it's the last one, but at this point they don't really believe it will ever end; unless -- until -- she dies. The horror of that thought is paralyzing.

The family decides to have her blessed by the ministers. They come to the house -- three of them in dark suits -- and they each lay a hand on the girl's head. The family does as well until there is a giant pyramid of hands on top of her head. The ministers close their eyes, mumble some words, and the family prays for a miracle.

The mother finds a doctor who finally listens and he starts treating the girl with gamma globulin shots and large doses of aspirin. She is taken twice a week to get a shot, crying each time.

The father moves out. They divorce. The sister tucks the girl into bed the first night he's gone. She plants a thousand kisses on the girl's neck; the girl squeals, drunk with laughter. The sister vows to come every night from now on, religiously.

Finally, finally, the girl gets better. By the time she is nearly five, she is well. She never again has the week-long fevers, the purple blotches, the overwhelming pain. Her finger and toes never again peel. She is a bit fragile, a bit frail, but she is well. She's now shy and careful around people; quiet, reserved; never wanting to make a scene or to stand out. Too much focus on her feels unbearable. She remembers her imaginary friends, but doesn't see them anymore. Did they only come to help her get well? She misses them.

As a teenager, she is introspective and feels unformed. She wonders if the sickness changed her into someone else. More than anything else, it feels odd to be herself; her body is such a stranger to her, such a traitor. Was she meant to die? She tries hard to no longer be a burden to her family. She very much wants to be unobtrusive, to be unnoticed, to be ordinary. Books become her refuge and her shield.

Kawasaki Disease began to emerge across all continents in the 1960s. Beginning in Japan, it was soon discovered in America. The cause is unclear. Typically patients are between six months and five years old. It is an acute febrile illness in which the walls of the blood vessels become inflamed. The symptoms include a high fever for at least 4 days; red mouth, tongue, and throat; abdominal, chest, head, and limb pain; bloodshot eyes; cool and clammy skin with discoloration and rash; and the peeling of the skin on the fingers and toes. Behavioral symptoms include night terrors, agitation, anxiety, and altered mental state. The duration of the active state is usually one week, once per month. Treatment is high doses of gamma globulin along with high doses of aspirin; antibiotics are not effective.

Lacy & THE KNIFE

by Eric Thralby

God put his hand into the earth and pulled out the sea. God put the birds in the trees and the cows in the fields. God put Lacy into a small blue house and across from her he put THE KNIFE. There are no answers except where we are put.

THE KNIFE crouched in the street over a large dying bat. Its cold eyes stared into the cold eyes of THE KNIFE.

"Is it already dead?" said Lacy, suddenly appearing as a shadow over THE KNIFE.

THE KNIFE indicated the blood on the pavement. The bat had crashed out of the sky.

Lacy frowned. "Pick it up," she said. "I think it will live."

THE KNIFE did not move but stayed crouched over the bat.

"We can save it, I said," said Lacy. "Pick it up."

THE KNIFE picked up the bat.

"I'm Lacy," Lacy said.

THE KNIFE shook Lacy's hand.

The street was very still. People watched from their windows. Why were two nine-year old girls alone and torturing a bat in the street?

"This is my room," Lacy said. She showed THE KNIFE around. "These are my books," she said. "Those are my clothes."

Lacy opened her closet. There was a fish tank. And inside the fish tank, a trout. It drifted there in the grey water of the tank, bubbles coming from its mouth, a wide eye, a wide jaw.

"Give me the bat," Lacy said.

THE KNIFE opened her hands.

The bat opened its wings and its neck creaked to look at them. It opened its mouth as if it were panting.

Lacy spread its wings and pinned it on the table. "Are you aware of what to do?" she said to THE KNIFE.

THE KNIFE reached into her pocket.

Night fell and Lacy and THE KNIFE ducked into the woods.

The girls found, through the trees, a pond. Beside the pond they set down their big black bag. The moon reflected in the pond. The pond smelled like rain.

"Are you really my friend?" asked Lacy.

THE KNIFE opened her own hand. And Lacy opened hers beside it.

A jogger jogged by.

They looked at him, mixing their blood together.

"What's in the bag?" he said.

"A dead body."

He left.

They held the bag over the water.

"Ready?" said Lacy.

One. Two.

They opened the bag. Nothing moved. They looked in the bag. The body of a trout. It opened its mouth. They set the bag into the pond. The bag spread in the water. Finally, the trout slipped slowly from the bag. The wings of a bat. It breathed in the water then flew down to the bottom of the pond.

"Did it drown?"

THE KNIFE's face remained as still and calm as the pond.

"But is it dead?"

It broke the surface and made an arc. It swam through the pond then shot out and flew into the trees.

Lacy went to chase after it. She ran through the trees. Then she stopped. Where was THE KNIFE?

Lacy returned to the pond.

THE KNIFE had thrown up. She sat wiping her mouth.

"Nerves," Lacy said.

THE KNIFE nodded.

Lacy held out her hand and helped THE KNIFE up.

In any neighborhood, there are wild ground creatures, wild tree creatures, wild pond creatures. Pet cats can wander off. Pet birds can go missing. But things also return.

And it's the same with human beings. Sometimes there are accidents. Sometimes things go wrong.

An arborist's hand was lost in the chipper. On the other end was just sawdust and blood, no fingers, no wrist.

Once the famous fat neighborhood cat disappeared. It was gone for three weeks, then finally returned. Its family found it in a box, chirping like a bird.

Raccoons, but nobody cares about them, crept through the trash in the darkness, stuffing their cheeks ballooned full of corncobs, not unlike squirrels.

A dog had been found. It had human fingers. And how do you explain that to a child? "Our dog is different now."

Once too THE KNIFE went missing.

The light in THE KNIFE's room did not come on for four days, nor did she appear at Lacy's house. THE KNIFE's parents were home. They wandered in and out of the house. Sometimes they carried in grocery bags. Sometimes they carried in giant bags made of fabric stuffed with things that might've been ordered in by THE KNIFE.

A week passed and THE KNIFE's window stayed dark.

Lacy couldn't take it anymore. She crossed the street to their house.

THE KNIFE's mother and father were in the front room crying. They took Lacy to THE KNIFE. She was alone in her room watching TV in the dark. Godzilla was breathing light and pulling a monster out of the sky.

"What's the matter with you?" said Lacy.

THE KNIFE did not get out of bed, but shot a finger up and jabbed it down to her abdomen.

"Are you dying or something?" said Lacy. She opened THE KNIFE's blinds. There was her own house, across the street.

THE KNIFE motioned to a nearby bucket which Lacy passed and THE KNIFE vomited into. THE KNIFE lay back in bed. She was pale and her hair stuck to her forehead.

These were the days the girls were still amateurs. Certainly, they were masters of appendages, but they knew nothing of the stuff inside the body.

THE KNIFE had not one but two abnormal kidneys. By

destiny, Lacy was a match.

Lacy lay in one hospital bed. And THE KNIFE lay in the other.

They would not go under at the same time, and so were given the option to watch the surgeries on small screens outside their operating rooms.

THE KNIFE watched the doctors cut open Lacy. Their knives were so incredibly sharp. Then when THE KNIFE went under, the screen was brought into Lacy, in her recovery bed. Still dreamy from being under the gas, Lacy watched the doctors use their instruments to disturb the order of THE KNIFE's internal organs. They cut out the old kidney and put in the new one. Now Lacy's kidney lived in THE KNIFE. Lacy felt her own scar, and the doctors rolled her back to bed.

It was a long recovery.

But soon enough they returned. And soon again began the neighbors' complaints: small shadows over their backyard fences and disappearances of cats.

One night in the woods, THE KNIFE was holding Lacy on her shoulders as Lacy coaxed a family of squirrels from a tree into a bag of McDonald's. THE KNIFE carved her name into the bark.

"Do you hear that?" said Lacy, THE KNIFE having finished K and gotten to N.

From total darkness, a sweet voice inched slowly and gently as honey through the thick of the woods.

Lacy jumped down. "What animal is that?" she said. "Don't you hear it?"

The voice grew louder, so the girls hid in the bushes.

It was as if a light was coming, a little girl their age coming through the woods in all white. She hummed and occasionally cupped her hands and called into the woods, "Snowy. Snowy."

She saw them through the bushes, like they weren't hidden at all. "What are you doing in the dark?" she said.

"Does she see us?" said Lacy.

"Yes," said the girl. She stood there very patiently. She wore a bonnet with a ribbon. "I'm looking for my cat. My name is Jessica. Can I use your phone?"

The girls walked through the woods together.

Dark trees bent over one another. Things moved around inside trees and other things crawled out. Something screamed then clamped open and shut in the hole of a trunk.

Pine needles fell slowly from the sky.

"What was that?" they said. They hid behind THE KNIFE.

In the darkness, the leaves were rustling. Something watched them.

Something leapt from the bushes. Lacy screamed.

But it was a cat. A beautiful cat with long white hair.

"Snowy," said Jessica. And the cat flew into her arms.

Jessica's eyes were like a doll's eyes.

But there is no limit to what you might improve.

Lacy showed Jessica around. "These are my CDs," she said. "These are my houseplants."

Snowy squirmed in Jessica's arms and Jessica set her down. Snowy followed after something into the hallway. THE KNIFE took her coat off and threw it on Lacy's floor.

"I want to show you this," said Lacy.

"What is it?" said Jessica.

"It's a crab," said Lacy.

Jessica whitened.

THE KNIFE opened her knife and deepened the K on Lacy's dresser.

"That's not a crab," said Jessica.

"Of course it's a crab," said Lacy.

"What's wrong?" said Jessica. "What's wrong with its eyes?"

"All the other crabs were picking on it. Because it only had one eye. But dog's eyes are really good. Dog's eyes see really far. Miss Anne's dog was getting old."

Jessica, like she would if she were on TV, clutched her hands over her mouth.

"What did you do to the dog," she whispered.

If people go missing, the police get involved. The police are not good or bad. But they really don't like it when people go missing.

When the police came to Lacy's house, Lacy and THE KNIFE were bandaging Lacy's hamster who had slipped up in its wheel.

"We're here on a missing person's report," said one cop named "DAVIS" who reminded THE KNIFE of her father.

Lacy led the cops into the kitchen and invited them to sit by a chocolate cake.

They declined.

She offered to boil water for tea.

They rubbed their bellies and declined.

"An arborist had to climb the tree and pull her down," said DAVIS.

"Up there for three nights," said the officer named BOB. "Up there screaming in that tree."

"Only until a jogger heard her and called the arborist," said Davis, "was she rescued down from that tree."

Snowy wandered in.

Snowy wrapped through the legs of the officers.

DAVIS reached down to pet Snowy. "She wandered up in that tree and got stuck," he said.

"Something's wrong with her now," said BOB.

THE KNIFE stopped cutting a slice from the cake.

"Wrong with her?" said Lacy.

BOB screwed up his face. He thought about it. "Wrong," he said. "Dead wrong. Something's wrong with her eyes."

Snowy stood to climb up on BOB so he picked her up and held her. Snowy bit BOB hard on the thumb.

BOB turned her around. Her eyes were closed tight. "What's wrong with your cat?" he said.

"There's nothing wrong with our cat," Lacy said.

"What's wrong with its eyes?" said BOB. "What's wrong with it?"

DAVIS came and looked at the cat. "Why won't it open its eyes?" he said.

Snowy opened its eyes. Its eyes were the eyes of a girl.

The state would say it was monstrous. The state would order separation. They would not be isolated together, away from the world, but separated and kept unbearably apart.

"THE KNIFE," said Lacy. "I want you to have this."

But Lacy had no gifts, only pointed at her heart.

The true expert of vivisection knows his masterpiece not when he sees that he has made the pig that can fly, nor when he sees that he has made the mouse that can speak. The true expert of vivisection knows his masterpiece only when he sees that he has made the pig see it must fly and the mouse that it must speak. Only by experiencing its own necessity, its own inseparability from wings or from voice, may the masterpiece reveal its true being and so reveal to the vivisectionist that the life he has created was essential all along.

THE KNIFE reached into her pocket.

In the time it took the state to file their warrant, Lacy and THE KNIFE, truly expert vivisectionists, conjoined two bodies into one.

Origin of Life - Rochelle Wong

Therapeutic Fantasy Epic

by Jonathan van Belle

A.

This is the suicide note of Cinderella of Phantásien. Imprisoned within this note, like the unopenable rebenok in a matryoshka doll, is a true story—with a true title: *Therapeutic Fantasy Epic.*

I toyed with different titles, such as *Visions of Hyperborea*—and throwaways: *Too Bitter and Impatient to Write*, *Another False Start*, *Restlessness*, *Breakdown Fantasy*, *Beyond the Fourth Wall*, and *Bastian Balthazar Bux at 35*. But I chose the most throwaway of these, the placeholder name of this word doc, a title I spun impromptu as a mission statement: *Therapeutic Fantasy Epic.*

This is a true fantasy, a chronicle of concrete, non-actual events. Everything happens at least once, my stepfather Kenny once said to me. This story happened *once upon a concrete, non-actual time.*

How do I know this? Depression. The seventh sense. Depression views the world-scenery from below and behind, sees the roots and the quiet capillary action of serotonin, oxytocin, endorphins, etc., the fairy sustainers of limb and leaf—of life's healthy mint, emerald, and shamrock greens. Depression sees fantasy everywhere and fantasizing everywhere; my black widow has such specialized pupils, eight black scrying pools to divine by dissociation the black light and nothing else. We eight eyes see all lies. Depression and fantasy are mother and daughter, with sixteen eyes between them.

As bonus evidence of this story's truth, this story, as I'll present it, was presented to me by the Egyptian goddess Sekhmet, who nightly moaned to me while I laid awake. She buzzed hatefully around my head. Sekhmet's lioness breath, pregnant with the perfume of soured blood, is hot on my face even now, hot with sacrificial demands, bestial revelations, laments, and—.

To the Savage God,

Ashley or Cinderella

B.

What, Sekhmet, will *our* fantasy be about? Perhaps it will be about a world where "insensate" fleshy clones can be printed easily and cheaply for customers, such that celebrities, one's coworkers—anyone whose DNA may be obtained—can be cloned and their insensate clone bodies "treated as one desires." Perhaps we follow a protagonist who fucks then eats his way through everybody he knows (their clone versions, that is). Towards the end, he hosts a dinner party where each guest is presented with a dish that is, unbeknownst to them, their own cloned flesh (which our protagonist carefully preserved). And he gleefully confesses "I've fucked all of you and eaten all of you. Fuck all of you! I've fucked you all in brutish ways! The standard orifices along with a few *new* ones."

Or, is that *too* savage?

Perhaps a fantasy about *endings*. Here is Henry. In his deepest temperament, he had relinquished, or perhaps unwillingly lost, his sense of buoyancy, of the propitious search for safe, buoyant, important things. That this buoyant sense was missing, that he felt the numb, rhythmic tug and nodded to the good sense, or at least the practicality, of the abyssal depths, did not stir anything in him. Some weights on his ankles, some bindings on his wrists, some opiates or dissociatives in his blood—technical preparations for a plunge, he imagined, sufficient for his purposes. The ocean at night seemed to him more appropriate; perhaps the sentiment was prompted by a dream he had suffered the week before, in which he felt uncomfortably warm as he gurgled downward; in this dream, the heat of the sun, not particularly its light, followed him to the abyssal plain, and even increased there on the blind, muddy floor, until the most intense heat gathered in the most intense pressure and stabilized into a state of perfect, boiling, airless equilibrium—as though he were stuck, without even the slightest millimeter of slack for relief, in a vast, pitch-black piece of smoldering glass. The ocean at night, then, seemed to him more appropriate—colder, softer, calmer, perhaps even thirst quenching, and, alas, absolutely bottomless—bottomless, he murmured, and allowed that final sound, that final word—*bottomless*—echo down the drain of his memories (most of which had little value or too much).

Yet a story about suicide is *too* "on the nose" for a suicide note. I need a girl sitting and watching a television show about zoo animals; when a giraffe appears, she crinkles her nose and asks her mom, "Is that like a camel?" I need a woman with a cup of tomato juice play-talking to a finch that perches on a branch above her; the finch darts off and the woman sips her juice, then rolls her left wrist to alleviate a dull pain in her hand. No. Nothing *in media res*. I need an *origin* story!

C.

Our fantasy begins as every fantasy begins: an author escaping itself. Into oceanic uncertainty, her skiff is cut free. He declares light, but what is light without anything else? With a shiver of cosmogonic morning energy, she begins to dictate: "The deeper dreamer interprets the interpretation of dreams and far less the dreams themselves." Then he erases those first missteps.

"Our dreams wash over with faces: faces with fingernails for teeth and toenails for eyes." No, he erases that too, then tries again: "I wish every art form, every medium, every instance of beauty, could rise all at once, in one infinite form, as one expression, and drown me." She erases that too.

Finally, now that he has cleared her conscience, acquiesced to his creative limits, doodled her worst efforts, he can finally, finally proceed to write her fantasy:

I can think of nothing more sublime than a universe coming to know itself, only to realize that it will lose itself, will forget itself entirely, will become "never was" and infinitely less—will slip from its own fading touch, to be nothingness again and eternally—to know: "I am this." And, without an answer from itself, from its own silent universal body, to die in the singularity of its own heart.

Do you hear the split of lyre strings? Do you see unfurled in royal ribbons our red volumes? We have no secret name, just a skiff that cuts no wake. No antechamber to blinkless beauty. No communion of family fumes. No pouring forth of returns. Therefore, why do you dwell on *the origin*? Do you wish to cradle in your arms your parents as newborns? Don't. Learn how to be an animal, banging quietly, gripped by a sorting machine and randomizer in a corner of Gloryland.

Baby Fever

by Mickey Collins

Abstract:
Is "baby fever" a real disease? Is there a ticking "biological clock"? After a close personal study of two subjects, the findings of this paper set out to prove that baby fever is indeed a real and also deadly disease. Symptoms of baby fever were found to include: a fever, sweating, swelling, paranoia, nesting, unease, slothfulness, increased sex drive, increased energy, talkativity, socializing, nagging, and more.

Limitations:
Every effort was taken to be impartial during this research, however as one of the subjects is also a co-author of this paper, impartiality cannot be assumed.

Methodology:
This research followed two subjects, one female and one male, over the course of seven years. Data was gathered through interviews, observation, and quantitative methods such as questionnaires.

Subject A: Twenty-something year old female
Subject B: Twenty-something year old male.

As Subject A's age neared 30 years old, she began to have increasingly positive reactions towards babies (see Fig. 1). At the beginning of the relationship with Subject B, when Subject A's age was closer to 20 years old, this was not the case.

An informal survey filled out by both subjects at the beginning of their adult lives ranked the importance of life events, such as having a career, having a baby, getting married, buying a house, etc. The survey was then repeated 7 years later, with Subjects closer to 30 years of age. The results of the first survey had "having a baby" toward the middle of both surveys filled out by the Subjects, though Subject A still had it ranked higher than Subject B. In the second survey, "having a baby" moved down the ranks for Subject B, but higher for Subject A.

Subject B experienced a steady disinterest in babies, and in fact had negative reactions at times. Subject B showed no signs of baby fever, despite his close proximity to the symptomatic Subject A. However, there is not enough evidence to say that it is not contagious, as Subject A was close with symptomatic female friends and family who had already had babies.

Each occurrence of a family member birthing another baby exponentially increased the amount of baby talk that Subject A subjected Subject B to. The amount of societal pressure increased with each "baby event" as well, with conversations from close family and friends such as, "When are you going to have a little one?" and "Where's my grandbaby?". There was a direct correlation between these baby talks with family and the amount of arguing between Subject A and Subject B (Fig. 2).

One positive outcome of these baby talks for Subject B was the increased sex drive realized in Subject A. With babies on the mind, Subject A was more willing to participate in sexual intercourse--usually unprotected--with Subject B (Figs. 3a, b, c, d, and e).

One unexpected result of increased sexual activity was an increase in "nagging," as nagging events were found to increase in parallel with sexual encounters. Subject A described the nagging as, "Nagging? What nagging? I gently prod until I get my way." Subject B described the nagging as, "A bloody screaming match that would wake the neighbors" and, "Yes, dear."

The baby fever increased to such a degree that Subject B worried Subject A would succumb to its deadly symptoms. Not willing to "go it alone," Subject B contracted Baby Fever as well.

Conclusion:
The only cure for Baby Fever is death. The death of a social life, the death of a sleep schedule, the death of any free time, and in rare cases the death of a relationship. These researchers hope to follow up with Subjects A, B, (and now, C) in seven years time.

The Fly

by Essam H. Al-Baqshi

translated from Arabic by Essam M. Al-Jassim

I was driving the other day, and the weather was getting hot, so I rolled up the window and turned on the air conditioning.

Nothing unusual happened until a fly inside the car began buzzing frenetically in all directions. As if that was not annoying enough, it began harassing me—a kiss on my cheek here, a smooch on my eyelid there. It even dared to smack me on the lips! I swung my hand rapidly back and forth to make the fly stay within the confines of etiquette and stop pestering me, but it only stalked me more persistently.

Exasperated by my vigorous hand waving, the fly attacked the steering wheel, causing me to swerve left and right as I tried to swat it, again and again, until I almost hit the sidewalk. I gripped the wheel firmly to foil the fly's miserable attempts. It grew bolder. Almost recklessly, it sat on my right thigh, then it moved to my left thigh. I became more suspicious, and doubts about the fly's intentions crowded my mind. I smelled a rat!

As I was trying to think of a way to rid myself of the audacious insect, I happened to drive past a massive emporium. I rolled down the window and indicated to the fly that the complex would be full of gorgeous ladies and handsome men. The winged bug immediately flew outside, heading towards the emporium.

Questions buzzed around my mind. Just questions …

Does this fly possess genes similar to those of humans? Do flies have an innate tendency to go after what looks good on the surface? Or was this merely the absurd act of a common insect?

Person-in-Hole

by L. Fid

There they were, finally, with a small sense of security. Approaching happiness, even, they sometimes ventured in cautious introspection.

Yes, that.

Incredible, after everything that happened.

They shook their head, not wishing to dwell on the past. They looked up and tracked a large bird sailing east above the trees. They skipped and whistled, eyes twinkling.

BAM.

They fall into a deep hole.

The more they try to escape, the more precarious their situation. The walls keep collapsing, burying them within mud, rocks.

They dig out a small space above their head and manage to keep it stable. A jagged patch of sky peers in. They can't move their body more than a few inches in most directions.

A spite of panic bubbles into their throat. They feel they might burst.

They focus past the roots, dirt, bugs and lock onto the grey light, back there, where they were, in the world. Not under it. They steady their breath.

Without realizing it, in moments too brief to count, their body tension deflates and unconsciousness rides in on vivid dream.

She was alone in a large gondola strung below a small

blimp. The craft sailed a few hundred feet above a tumultuous seascape, buffeted by occasional side winds, driven forward by an immense storm front, which she could hear and feel as a gut-churning rumble. She sat cross-legged on the thatched wire floor, watching the waves below.

The gondola was open at the top except for some support beams, but she dared not stand to peer over the rails. The floor was tilted towards the front at a steep pitch, such was the fierce velocity, and the whole structure, including the dark cloth above, convulsed and trembled periodically.

The floor seemed sturdy enough and she kept it close. In the diamond-shaped openings between the steel grate, the swelling sea did not seem so reassuring. Soon enough, the swells bunched together, then crested and crashed in lines as a frothy spray shot up. The blimp continued apace, first over earthen berms of giant rocks and concrete, then land. Warehouses, parking lots, building rooftops and city streets passed beneath.

Still, she felt unprepared when a large glass office building slid beside, towering above. A jolt of recognition rang through her as the blimp decreased its speed and began to deftly navigate the city streets.

The gondola resumed a proper horizontal. She stood, put her hands on the rail, examined her office clothes beneath the translucent rain gear.

A rope uncoiled beneath the floor towards the skyways and streets below. It caught and the blimp spiraled into a three-story open bay carved out of the side of an old skyscraper. Amid an ornate panoply of statuary and colonnade, fountains and ferns, veranda and terraces, a patio spun out to receive them.

Two other blimps were waiting, empty, on similar patios tucked away to the side of the bay. The rope was pulled taught, the floor magnetically locked, the blimp partially deflated and the gondola's side folded out. She stepped confidently onto the polished stone. Two revolving doors turned slowly against the wall. She approached the left. The door's turning quickened to match her pace.

Once inside, she turned her jaw at the air pressure change, paused for her eyes to adjust. The elevator's doors were just starting to close across the crowded foyer. She dodged past knots of fellow commuters and got a hand within in time to cease the shutting. Amid some murmured moans, she packed herself inside the flesh can. She grabbed a handstrap just as the floor fell, gravity dropped, and they ascended together.

They kick their knee, once, twice. No resistance. A short debate, then down they go, into the hole their body had found. After some rooty tendrils, the tunnel opens and... there they are.

Themselves. Breathing -- and seeing, even. Yes!

The walls are luminescent, or so it seems. The whole shebang might crumble and suffocate them at any second, but... There they are!

A few beats later, their confidence subsides and the path seems uncertain. The tunnel twists to the side, and, buttressed by a large boulder, narrows to a dark squeeze. Who's to say what's on the other side? When and why? Not to mention, where and what? What.

What? What is the question, so they thought.

Fingers, caressing digits, acting with purpose and love... They are there. Then everywhere. They pull themself down, inside and, down. They fall. A cavern, and there they are! They float before the assembled moalstirps.

The moalstirps' bodies are huge and, by contrast, they -- they are nothing, a thin strip. They dangle, wobbling in place, prostate, amid a sphere of greater being. A moalstirp approaches, with some of the luminescent wall in its beak. The giant carefully places the glowing debris onto the strip. On me.

The process continues a hundred fold and I am created. I

am not of the earth. I am. I am it. I am the earth.

When they deem me done, I swing my appendages back and forth, gleefully. New tissue and sinew -- strong, honed, ready. I breaststroke through the hall, then dive into the dark earth, easily passing through the rocky soil.

I swim round and round, warmly welcomed into each alcove as I tour this small slice of the great moalstirp strata. Still, I'm drawn to surface. Hindered by greater resistance the higher I get, I claw my way forward. I choke, fear I will not make it.

Digits reach for me, grasp my head, pull me out. The world rings loudly as I crawl into a bright alien world. Masked monsters hover over me, inspecting.

Word Origins
by Desiree Ducharme

The lipstick was gross. Sticky yet dry, a bitter wax in 'Fire Engine Red.' It was orange. I was an expert on Orange thanks to my gang on The Street. Grover and John-John did a side by side analysis of red to orange just this morning. The lipstick was orange. Miss Not-the-Teacher was instructing me to kiss the paper, "with your mouth." She is making weird shapes with her mouth as she says, "mouth" and pointing to the center of the page. There were a lot of rules about where one should and shouldn't put their mouth. Paper was on the "no" list. I was only three but I knew you weren't supposed to put paper in your mouth. Between her insistence that the lipstick is red and wanting me to put my mouth on paper, Miss Not-the-Teacher was losing credibility by the second. How does Bizzy stay here with this strange woman?

"Just kiss the paper and I'll wipe it off!" I quickly touched the paper with my orange wax coated lips. The paper stuck. Neat. Miss Not-the-Teacher pulled it off. She replaces it with sandpaper disguised as a napkin. I quickly ducked her second attempt at assault by wiping my mouth on my sleeve. Sleeves were also on the "no" list but I was against this whole operation from the beginning. Miss Not-the-Teacher was the captain here and we were clearly adrift. I stare at the orange-not-red imprint of my mouth above the letters m,o,u,t, and h. Something is happening here. I sensed there is something she is trying to tell me. That this whole thing is about more than lipstick and where we put our mouths. Mouths hold our taste sense. My Mouth. Miss Not-the-Teacher takes my Senses Train away for gluing.

It is lay-on-the-floor-quiet-and-still-until-your-mom-comes o'clock. I use this time to prepare my answers for mom. She is very interested in what I learn at pre-school. I'm not sure what I'm supposed to be learning but she asks so I like to have an answer ready for her. It keeps the conversation moving as we navigate Stumps Market.

Today I learned:

We have five senses, most of which are part of our face. Some are in our hands and we must keep our hands to ourselves, especially Billy. - Mom will like this answer.

Miss Not-the-Teacher is not to be trusted. Doesn't know red from orange. Lies about lipstick. Makes questionable choices about where to put one's mouth. - Mom might worry about this one.

Lipstick is gross and should be avoided. - Ask Mom why lipstick is a thing.

Bizzy is down for second-nap. I tried to ask her about preschool after Stumps but she didn't want to talk about it. Mom is also down for second-nap. My gang was on TV. The monsters were vomiting letters. A 'c' dropped from one of them. An 'a' and a 't' popped out of the other. The monster who dropped the 'c' made a ka-sound. I make a ka-sound. The monster who dropped the 'a' & 't' said, "at." I say at. They pushed their letters together and made their sounds faster. The 'c' lit up.

C

The 'a' and 't' lit up.

AT

c…at

c..at

cat

A small cat sat above the letters and meowed. Something deep in the center of me cracks like lightning. The letters! C-A-T. CAT. Cat! This is what Ernie and the monsters had been trying to tell me this whole time. I ran to our books screaming, "CAT!" There it was on the cover of "The Cat in the Hat." I flipped every page. There! Cat. I knew this story because my mom read us all the Doctor's work. C (ka) at (at), CAT. Oh my god. H (huh) at (at), HAT. HAT! Pat, sat, sit, fan, ran, sad, mad, bad! I was freaking out.

"Mooooommmmmm! Mom, the letters! The LETTERS!!! CAT. MOM! CAT!"

"Wha!? Are you hurt?! Did you see a cat, sweetie?"

"Yes. I see a cat. C and A and T. Cat, mom, it's the letters! The letters together are cat!"

"Oh, yes. Can we read later? I thought you were sleeping? Is Bizzy awake?"

"No. She's asleep still. Mom, listen, the monsters, I figured it out! They've been trying to tell me this whole time and I get it!"

"That's nice. Is Sesame Street on?"

"Oh, it's on." and I was awake.

First, There Was The Void

by Azalea Micketti

First, there was the Void.

And the Great Mother swam through the sea of nothing and was cradled by the Void. And the Void sang to Her. The Mother described the Void, and all the infinite they contained. And their love was eternal because there was no time and so everything was endless.

The Great Mother sang, and from Her lips tumbled stars and clouds and moons and countless facets of light. They fell and were caught by the Void, who drank them in. And so the Mother was everything and the Void was nothing.

And the Mother created the island and called it Tiullu, where She planted trees and created streams and mountains. And She gave life to the creatures of the land and the air and the mosses on the trees, decorating the world She built so She might give it to the Void. And the Void smiled smiled with no face.

And the Void, having nothing to gift the Mother in return, transformed the stars into spun sugar filaments of joy and pain. And they fed these to the Mother by theirher own hand.

The Mother was fed, and She became full of these stars. She carried them in Her womb until they grew strong and resonant and She could no longer contain them. And so She fractured into thirteen. One for each of the twelve stars and one for Herself.

And in the rupture, the Children of the Stars—who were called the Urdei—were scattered across the sky and across the land. And twelve Urdei came to land on Tiullu, but the Thirteenth was lost. No one knows where the Thirteenth Fragment lies, the last fragment of the Mother Herself.

The Void cried out at this great loss, the soundless notes of their grief caught in the space where there is no time, echoing for eternity.

And still the Void is searching.

*

And so the twelve fragments came to Tiullu, the place their Mother had created. And there they found all that the Mother had wrought, and the Void had transformed. And for a time the Urdei were happy. They learned to create, as the Great Mother had before them. And to transform, as the Void forever will. And they learned of each other and how they were different and the same.

And they stayed on the island of Tiullu for many aeons, creating and transforming and destroying. Until one of the Urdei came to their siblings and sang, i am. And the other Urdei, unaware that they might Be outside of Themselves, were confused and afraid. But then the Uei sang again, I am. And with a ringing voice they sang, I Am. And for the first time the Urdei saw themselves as they saw each other. They understood that they might act as individuals and for their own delights. And that first Uei called themself Getex, the Traveler, and they were the first to leave Tiullu.

And for many more aeons Getex walked, and as they walked the world appeared. And as they walked the world transformed. And as they walked the world was destroyed. And they learned many new things, and came to know themself. And at last it came time to return to Tiullu.

And as Getex stepped into the ocean, there appeared to them one of the Urdei. And Getex greeted them with great joy, and the Uei returned the greeting and called themself Fiunduinu, the Ferryman. And Fiunduinu took Getex back to Tiullu, where they were greeted by their siblings.

Getex sat upon the sand and told the Urdei of their journey. Of the passage of time, and the seasons, and the animals and the land. And as they shared these things, images appeared in the minds of the other Urdei and there was a great longing to see for themselves.

But when the other Urdei tried to leave Tiullu, they discovered they were not able to. And when Getex, the Traveler, again left Tiullu they did not return for another lifetime, when again they were greeted by Fiunduinu upon their return.

This time the Urdei were angry. "Take us with you!" they cried, but Getex did not know how. Then, quietly as she did everything, the Uei who called herself Unstox, the Gardner, stepped forward. She cared more for the plants of the earth and the animals that lived upon it than for anything else. And in her quiet voice, as gentle as the whispering wind, she told her siblings of what she had created.

For she more than others had seen what their Mother had left, and knew that there was more to create. And so she had made new plants and animals, some who lived upon the land, and some in the sea, and even others who floated through the air. And all around her was the sparkle of her creation, and the echo of the Great Mother's song.

And the Urdei gathered round and saw that from the earth of Tiullu and the water of the sea, Unstox had made a new creature: the human. And the Urdei learned that though they could not yet leave Tiullu as Getex could, they were able to see through the eyes of these new creatures and experience new things. And so Unstox, the Gardner, taught the Urdei how to make their own, and they each took offo the earth and of the sea and made a human.

And so they sent these humans off into the world, giving them boats to sail and knowledge of the plants and the animals. And the humans were gone for many years, and through their eyes the Urdei were able to see the world for themselves. And through the humans they learned the world moved differently beyond Tiullu. It was always changing, and time was measured in cycles and lines, not as a single never-ending moment.

And the passage of time affected the humans differently than it did the Urdei. And when the humans finally returned to Tiullu they showed signs of age, and it was not long after that their bodies returned to the earth and ocean from whence they came. And Unstox wept for these her fallen creations, but she also sang in praise for they had experienceds a cycle unlike any she had ever known.

And so the Urdeio created more humans and sent them into the world. But not all returned before their bodies succumbed to the passage of time. But those that were still animate sent their comrades afloat so that Fiunduinu might collect them and bear them back to Tiullu that they might be transformed. And some did not return at all. And when the Urdei looked out into the world they saw that the humans had themselves created more humans, and begun to live upon the land beyond Tiullu.

And there were some Urdei who were content to sit upon the Island of Tiullu and watch, experiencing the world through the eyes of their human creations. And there were some who felt that it was only right that they themselves experience the world firsthand. And there were some who learned, as Getex had before them, that they might leave Tiullu but that to do so was to lose themselves in the river of time until Fiunduinu, the Ferryman, came to fetch them again.

At long last it was the Twins, Trado & Tradat (who were as one until they split themselves in half that together they might experience their own duality), who noticed that the humans in the world remembered them, and gave them praise and gifts as their Mother had the Void. And these gifts gave them strength. And with this newfound strength they were able to travel into the world without a human vessel. And they learned that there were places in the world where they might dwell easier than others. And there were humans who prepared the way for them, and whose gifts continued to strengthen them as they dwelt among them.

But soon they found that in their time beyond Tiullu, the humans had multiplied and changed. They had learned how to communicate with each other in a way the Urdei could not: with words and gestures instead of light and harmony. And the humans themselves gained strength from the land and the water, and comfort from the stories they told each other of Tiullu and the Urdei who lived upon it.

The Urdei found they also gained strength from these stories, and with the help of the one they called Haudquix, the Weaver, learned to influence the dreams and the visions of these humans that they might tell more stories. And the humans sang the praises of the Urdei and learned new stories to tell. And as the Urdei drank in their words they passed along their own gifts to those humans whom they favored.

And the Urdei, who were new to the world but had existed for many millennia, taught the humans new things. They taught them methods of sailing upon the ocean, and seeing the places in the Void where the Urdei themselves had once dwelt. And with this knowledge the humans were able to travel even farther upon the ocean.

But there was one of the Urdei who did not feel content upon Tiullu or traveling in the world. Eriunleue, the Star, the last one to fall upon Tiullu, dreamed of the endless empty of the Void and once more greeting the Thirteenth Fragment. And so she sought a way off Tiullu and into the sky. She searched and searched until she came upon a mountain so high it scraped the firmament above. And when she stood upon the top with fingers outstretched she was able to grasp the trailing cloak of the Void as they passed by. And so she becaome the only Uei to return to the sky and to the Void, and the only star to shine down upon the world.

Another of the Urdei, naive and unaware, sent humans to sail upon the sea with no knowledge to guide them. These humans were soon lost, and she was stricken with grief at what she had done. She began to churn the ocean, looking for the lost ones, but they were not found. Uunwilling to abandon hope she hurtled herself into the sky until she could hover above the land and ocean and see all that had been lost. She pulled at the waters of the sea, hoping to unearth the humans she had so recklessly abandoned. But they did not appear. Soon her strength began to wane and she became exhausted. Gathering herself into a fold of the Void's midnight cloak she hid her face and slept.

The humans, having become accustomed to her shining face above them each night, became afraid. And they sang songs and made offerings and lit fires in an attempt to strengthen her so she might shine again. Eventually the gifts and the blessings caught her attention and she unwound her shroud. Seeing the joy her presence brought she was once more struck with the sorrow of those who had been lost. And so she searched again, pulling the tides in and out, in and out, washing exhausted travelers to shore, but never finding those who had been hers. And thereafter she was called Onin, the Moon.

And as the Urdei grew in strength they traveled farther into the world, until none were left on the Island of Tiullu but Unstox, the Gardner, and Fiunduinu, the Ferryman. And Fiunduinu continued to bring the humans back to Tiullu where Unstox continued to transform them into earth and ocean that she might create more life.

And Getex continued to walk many lifetimes over, always returning to Tiullu when they found themselves once more.

Until they did not.

Bios

Essam M. Al-Jassim

I am a writer and translator. I have a bachelor's degree in Foreign Languages and Education from King Faisal University, Hofuf. My translations appear in a variety of online and print Arabic and English literary journals. I live in Hofuf, Saudi Arabia.

Roger Camp

Roger Camp is the author of three photography books including the award-winning *Butterflies in Flight* (Thames & Hudson, 2002) and *Heat* (Charta, Milano, 2008). His work has appeared in numerous journals including *The New England Review*, *New York Quarterly*, and the *Vassar Review*. He previously worked as a reference librarian at the Santa Ana Public Library and as an analytical bibliographer for the director of the Humanities Research Center at the University of Texas, Austin.

Mickey Collins

~~Mickey rights wrongs~~. ~~Mickey wrongs rites~~. Mickey writes words, sometimes wrong words but he tries to get it write.

Ben Crowley

Ben Crowley is from Pittsburgh, Pennsylvania. He is happy to get back to writing because he has already paid a kidney, a finger and a thumb to *Deep Overstock* and is considering dishing out three molars. Ben used to sort books for the Amazon warehouse, in our beautiful backcountry of western Pittsburgh. Now he drives a truck, but he's still selling books at whatever diner, truckstop or seedy hotel he finds himself in.

Amanda Depperschmidt

Amanda Depperschmidt is a laid-off bookseller from the PPR zone at Powell's City of Books. Her writing focuses on archival theory, climate destruction, and animals.

Desiree Ducharme

Desiree Ducharme spends her days imagining pleasant and unpleasant nonsense then writing it down. During her semi-voluntary, health-adjacent, potentially-permanent sabbatical from her dream job as a Used Book Buying Dragon at Powell's City of Books, has freed up a lot of her time. She washed her dreams and became a writer. You can find more of her work at her website.

Robert Eversmann
Robert Eversmann works for Deep Overstock. His website is roberteversmann.com

L. Fid
L. Fid is a member of a pseudonymous arts collective dedicated to world domination.

Dianah Hughley
Dianah Hughley has been a bookseller for Powell's Books since 2008. She mainly writes staff pick reviews, so this essay is a big stretch for her. She works in the blue room and specializes in literary and Pacific Northwest fiction. She lives in Portland with her husband and many, many -- too many -- books.

Erin Karbuczky
Erin Karbuczky is a Lead Bookseller at Powell's Books, and an avid reader and book collector. Her mission as a bookseller is to unite each person with the perfect book for them, so that they may grow to love reading as much as she does. She resides in the Pacific Northwest with her husband, their cat, and a head full of stories aching to share with the world.

Ariel Kusby
Ariel Kusby is a writer and bookseller based in Portland, Oregon. She currently works in the Rose and Orange rooms at Powell's City of Books, where she pays special attention to children's books about witches, odd cookbooks, and gnome gardening guides. You can check out her writing at www.arielkusby.com.

Azalea Micketti
Azalea is a writer, director, actor, and bookseller living in the weirdest place on earth (open for heated discussion). She loves words, knows a little too much about Shakespeare, and will happily discuss books for literal hours.

Timothy Arliss O'Brien
Timothy Arliss O'Brien is an interdisciplinary artist in music composition, writing, and visual arts. His goal is to connect people to accessible new music that showcases virtuosic abilities without losing touch of authentic emotions. He has premiered music with The Astoria Music Festival, Cascadia Composers, Sound of Late's 48 hour Composition Competition

and ENAensemble's Serial Opera Project. He also wants to produce writing that connects the reader to themselves in a way that promotes wonder and self realization. He has published several novels (*Dear God I'm a Faggot, They*), and has written for Look Up Records (Seattle), Our Bible App, and *Deep Overstock: The Bookseller's Journal.* He has also combined his passion for poetry with his love of publishing and curates the podcast The Poet Heroic. He also showcases his makeup skills as the phenomenal drag queen Tabitha Acidz.

Check out more of his writing, and his full discography at his website: www.timothyarlissobrien.com

NAT PW

Nat PW is a storyteller, painter, performance artist, book collector, bird watcher, list maker.

MICHAEL SANTIAGO

Michael Santiago is a serial expat, avid traveler, and writer of all kinds. Originally from New York City, and later relocating to Rome in 2016 and Nanjing in 2018. He enjoys the finer things in life like walks on the beach, existential conversations and swapping murder mystery ideas. Keen on exploring themes of humanity within a fictitious context and aspiring author.

BOB SELCROSSE

Bob Selcrosse grew up with his mother, selling books, in the Pacific Northwest. He is now working on a book about a book. It is based in the Pacific Northwest. The book is *The Cabinet of Children.*

JIHYE SHIN

Jihye Shin is a 1.5-generation Korean-American bookseller in Florida. Her work focuses on the poetics of the analog-digital, liminial and futurist differences. She is also the creator of a text-based interactive game called Goodnight, Starlight. Her professional website is www.jihyeshin.ink.

E.T. STARMANN

E.T. Starmann is a pulp fanatic. Although he may not be a professional bookseller or librarian, he is a long-time Weird Tales, Amazing Stories, All-Story collector. A Portland native, E.T. has spent countless hours in the Gold Room nook at Powell's, pouring through the latest pulp rack covers. E.T.'s work is heavily inspired by Lloyd Arthur Eshbach, Robert E Howard and Edgar Rice Burroughs.

Adam Stewart
AS is a poet, writer, chess-player, and a future physician. He enjoys writing poems in his spare time that are both intimate and expansive. He currently resides in NYC.

Sue Su
Sue Su is a Cambridge CELTA-qualified teacher with fluent English and Mandarin currently teaching Mandarin as a modern foreign language in the British School of Nanjing whilst tutoring English and Chinese privately.

Eric Thralby
Captain by trade, Cpt. Eric Thralby works wood in his long off-days. He time-to-time pilots the Bremerton Ferry (Bremerton—Vashon; Vahon—Bremerton), while other times sells books on amazon.com, SellerID: plainpages. He'll sell any books the people love, strolling down to library and yard sales, but he loves especially books of Romantic fiction, not of risqué gargoyles, not harlequin romance, but knights, errant or of the Table. Eric has not published before, but has read in local readings at the Gig Harbor Candy Company and the Lavender Inne, also in Gig Harbor.

Jonathan van Belle
Jonathan van Belle is a copy editor for Outlier.org, an online education platform. He previously worked as a bookseller at Powell's City of Books. Jonathan is the author of several books, all available online, and is currently working on his first book for Deep Overstock Publishing.

ZB Wagman
ZB Wagman is a writer based in Portland, Oregon. When not writing, he spends his days working at the Beaverton City Library.

Nicholas Yandell
Nicholas Yandell is a composer, who sometimes creates with words instead of sound. In those cases, he usually ends up with fiction and occasionally poetry. He also paints and draws, and often all these activities become combined, because they're really not all that different from each other, and it's all just art right?
When not working on creative projects, Nick works as a bookseller at Powell's Books in Portland, Oregon, where he enjoys being surrounded by a wealth of knowledge, as well as working and interacting with creatively stimulating people. He has a website where he displays his creations; it's nicholasyandell.com. Check it out!

www.ingramcontent.com/pod-product-compliance
Lightning Source LLC
Chambersburg PA
CBHW032040180726
48284CB00008B/2674
* 9 7 8 1 9 4 9 1 2 7 1 5 7 *